CURRY
FAMILY
BIOGRAPHIES

Thompson Family History Biographies

Vol. 5, Ed. 1

We're all ghosts.

We all carry, inside us, people who came before us

- Liam Callanan

Genealogy of Mazo/Mason, Brown (2), Thompson (2), Shatteen, Morgan, Forsythe, Hampton, Washington, Robinson, Curry, Glover, Frazier et al of Nassau, Bahamas; Chatham, Jefferson & Washington Counties, GA; and Allendale, Barnwell & Beaufort Counties, SC

Marc D. Thompson
& Jack Butler

Cover Photograph:

Delores Ann Curry, mother-in-law of author.

Family histories require constant revision.

Please contact author with any corrections or additions,

at info@marcdthompson.net.

Published by:

VirtuFit Delray Beach, FL

www.marcdthompson.net

info@marcdthompson.net

ISBN: 978-0990807445

OTHER BOOKS BY AUTHOR

Armstrong Family History, © 2013

Biographies of our Maternal Family History, Coming Soon

Biographies of our Paternal Family History, © 2015

Biographies of the Anderson Family Genealogy, © 2014

Biographies of the Batdorf Family Genealogy, © 2014

Biographies of the Duncan Family Genealogy, © 2014

Biographies of the Thompson Family Genealogy, © 2015

Compendium of Virtual and Traditional Fitness, © 2015

Fitness Book of Lists, © 2012

Fitness Quotes of Humorous Inspiration, © 2011

Genealogy of Anderson, Keefer, Gaugler, Livezly..., © 2014

Genealogy of Batdorf, Wert, Peters, Row..., © 2013

Genealogy of Duncan, Layman, McCloud, Overlander..., © 2014

Genealogy of Thompson, Hensel, Goodman, Updegrove..., © 2013

Mazo & Curry Family History, © 2010

Mower Family History, Coming Soon

Photographic Family History, Coming Soon

Poems...Of Eternal Moments, © 2012

Romano & O'Connor Family History, © 2012

Romano Family Biographies, © 2014

Thompson Family History, © 2014

Virtual Personal Training Manual, © 2013

Wittle & Acri Family History, © 2011

Wittle Family Biographies, Coming Soon

DEDICATION

This volume is dedicated to all *our family and friends*, who selflessly donated information, time, effort, research and love to make this compilation possible.

ACKNOWLEDGMENTS

Thanks to my parents, my sisters, and my children for the knowledge and support. Thanks to my history teachers through high school and college. Thanks to Ray from Pennsylvania State Library and Gary Rosenberg for their tutelage. Special thanks to the writing talents of Jack Butler. Thanks to my hundreds of cousins, near and far, who have donated their time as well as their long-toiled family histories. Thanks to every clerk, registrar, cemetery manager, LDS employee, ancestry.com staff and others who researched in places I couldn't visit. This book is truly the love of thousands

CONTENTS

FOREWORD

by Melvalean Thompson (1967-2008)

Heaven sent down your love

And you gave it to me

Heaven gave you that heart

And you gave it to me

Your love is supreme

How can I love you any less

This was written by our sweet Mel on December 8, 2000, and serves as a perfect foreword to the strength and perseverance of those who came before and for those who come after her.

PROLOGUE

by Marc D. Thompson

If I were given the opportunity to live in any era, I would most certainly pick the 1870s. The time was simple and the people were honest. Folks worked hard and took pride in their families, their homes and their reputations. When I look into the eyes of our ancestors from that time period, I feel a link; I would have fit nicely in their time.

Who we are cannot be separated from where we're from.
- Malcolm Gladwell

INTRODUCTION

Genealogy is a lifelong duty. The day we were born or the day we bore children ourselves, we gained a responsibility of passing along our history. We are responsible for the knowledge of our parents and of our grandparents and all the wisdom that comes with this knowledge. Our duty, therefore, includes our children's heritage—including the names and faces of our forefathers and mothers, the medical history and genetic backgrounds of their blood lines, the princes and the paupers, the photographs and historical places, the tragedies and the joys.

The ancient Scottish bards similarly memorized their royal families, reciting the pedigrees of the Old Scot's Kings regardless of the complexity. The Irish kings would pass down their regal history orally. They would recite a list of names—their kin—noting outstanding events associated with the forbearers. West African families passed down stories from generation to generation. On and one with the mnemonic Peruvians, the beaded of New Zealand, the Indian Cera Kings, the extensive Chinese genealogies, the ancient Japanese string of names. Argument could be said that ALL family have the need for knowledge of their genealogy.

Genealogy was created in order for people to know the history of their lineage, to discover their origins, and to prove blood-lines and royalty. This volume was compiled in response to our deep desire to understand and discover their past. It shall stand as part of the legacy of our ancestry. Our ancestors had wisdom and understanding. They had goals, glories, and personalities.

Our 35-year journey has led to the numerous genealogy volumes and updates of previous volumes. In most cases, the Anglicized first and middle names were used throughout the Narrative. For example, Johann Heinrich is John Henry and Orsala Francesca is Ursula Frances. The most commonly found surname was used, whether

Anglicized or not. The majority of the collateral information was derived from the U.S. Census records and data from cousins' compilations.

Additionally, place names were documented as precisely as possible, using the name of the place as it was at that time in history. For example, parts of Germany were once Prussia, parts of Lebanon County, Pennsylvania were once Lancaster County, Pennsylvania. However in some cases, the common name was used. Before Pennsylvania's statehood, although it was the Swedish Colony and later the Province of Pennsylvania, however simply Pennsylvania was used. Lastly, to preserve privacy, all information on living persons has been removed or privatized.

Many genealogies tend to trace a descendant line or the paternal line (single ascendancy). Our purpose was to trace all ancestors with equal perseverance back in time. This is a monumental—if not near impossible—task. We have compiled a pedigree, beginning with our children and with the current emphasis on generations one through ten, although we have completed research as far back as generation 21. Additional collateral ancestor's data have begun to be added as of 2015.

The mission of our genealogy books is four-fold. First, to amass photographs—as a face can tell a thousand tales—as so much can be learned from them. The second goal is to document the medical background of our ancestors, so our children can lead a healthier life. The third goal is to continue to extend the lineage in order to link to as many relatives as possible. Our final goal leads us to the building of narratives from this amassed information, producing a readable experience of our ancestors and their lives. Our ancestors are not mere names or dates—they have tales to tell, journeys to document, lives to discover. They have accomplishments and setbacks, which in turn help us with ours. As we mentioned "Who we are cannot be separated from where we're from," this book therefore allows us to know precisely where we're from.

Chapter 1:
GENERATION ONE
What's In a Name

Fame is the inheritance not of the dead, but of the living.
It is we who look back with lofty pride to
the great names of antiquity.
- William Hazlitt

Our children, as with all life, represent the beginning of all things. They are bore and they begin their life-long experiences. Here they are the beginning of our book, back from which we narrate to bring their ancestors to life. Our children, nephews and nieces were all born from 1980–2010. Here are some of the meanings behind our children's names and some interested genealogy facts.

Adam: This is the Hebrew word for "man." It could be ultimately derived from Hebrew Adam meaning "to be red," referring to the ruddy color of human skin, or from Akkadian adamu meaning "to make." According to Genesis in the Old Testament Adam was created from the earth by God. There is a word play on Hebrew adamah meaning "earth." He and Eve were supposedly the first humans, living happily in the Garden of Eden until Adam ate a forbidden fruit given to him by Eve. As an English Christian name, Adam has been common since the Middle Ages, and it received a boost after the Protestant Reformation. A famous bearer was Scottish economist Adam Smith.

Andrew: English form of the Greek name Andreas, which was derived from andreios "manly, masculine," a derivative of aner "man." In the New Testament the apostle Andrew, the first disciple to join Jesus, is the brother of Simon Peter. According to tradition, he later preached in the Black Sea region, with some legends saying he was crucified on an X-shaped cross. Andrew, being a Greek name, was probably only a nickname or a translation of his real Hebrew name, which is not known. This name has been common throughout the Christian world, and it became very popular in the Middle Ages. Saint Andrew is regarded as the patron of Scotland, Russia, Greece and Romania. The name has been borne by three kings of Hungary, American president Andrew Jackson and, more recently, English composer Andrew Lloyd Webber.

Ashley: From an English surname which was originally derived from place names meaning "ash tree clearing," from Old English Aesc and Leah. Until the 1960s it was more commonly given to boys in the United States, but it is now most often used on girls.

Connor: Anglicized form of the Gaelic name Conchobhar which means "dog lover" or "wolf lover." It has been in use in Ireland for centuries and was the name of several Irish kings. It was also borne by the legendary Ulster King Conchobar mac Nessa, known for his tragic desire for Deirdre.

Marie: French and Czech form of Maria. A notable bearer of this name was Marie Antoinette, a queen of France, and Marie Curie, a physicist and chemist who studied radioactivity with her husband Pierre. Latin form of Greek from Hebrew Mary. Maria is the usual form of the name in many European languages, as well as a secondary form in other languages such as English. In some countries, for example Germany, Poland and Italy, Maria is occasionally used as a masculine middle name. This was the name of two ruling queens of Portugal. It was also borne by the Habsburg queen Maria Theresa, whose inheritance of the domains of her father, the Holy Roman Emperor Charles VI, began the War of the Austrian Succession. The meaning is not known for certain, but there are several theories including "sea of bitterness," "rebelliousness," and "wished for child." However it was most likely originally an Egyptian name, perhaps derived in part from my "beloved" or my "love."

Renae: French form of Renatus. A famous bearer was the French mathematician and rationalist philosopher René Descartes. Late Latin name meaning "born again."

Roman: From the Late Latin name Romanus which meant "Roman."
Sophia: Means "wisdom" in Greek. This was the name of an early, probably mythical, saint who died of grief after her three daughters were martyred. Legends about her probably arose as a result of a medieval misunderstanding of the phrase Hagia.

Rachel: From the Hebrew name רָחֵל (Rachel) meaning "ewe." In the Old Testament this is the name of the favorite wife of Jacob and the mother of Joseph and Benjamin. The name was common among Jews in the Middle Ages, but it was not generally used as a Christian name in the English-speaking world until after the Protestant Reformation.

Sophia: "Holy Wisdom," which was the name of a large basilica in Constantinople. This name was common among continental European royalty during the Middle Ages, and it was popularized in Britain by the German House of Hanover when they inherited the British throne in the 18th century. It was the name of characters in the novels Tom Jones by Henry Fielding and The Vicar of Wakefield by Oliver Goldsmith.

Tiffany: Medieval form of Theopania. This name was traditionally given to girls born on the Epiphany (January 6), the festival commemorating the visit of the Magi to the infant Jesus. The name died out after the Middle Ages, but it was revived by the movie *Breakfast at Tiffany's*, the title of which refers to the Tiffany's jewelry store in New York.

Tyler: From an English surname meaning "tiler of roofs". The surname was borne by American president John Tyler.

Through the research of the TFH, we have discovered that we are related to some famous and infamous folks, and even found that there are some areas of the world named for our distant families. We are direct-line descendants of William Duke of Jülich-Cleves-Berg and Maria of Austria, Duchess of Jülich-Cleves-Berg, Countess Clothilde de Valois de Reni and Jacques de Sellaire, Von Zeller of Castle Zellerstein of Zurich, John Thomson of Haddington, Johann La Hentzelle of Lorraine, General John Benfield of Normandy, Henri Banage de Beauval of Rouen, Alexander Thompson of Schuylkill, the Guerne family of Eschert, the Bager family of Wiesbaden, the Emmerich family of Delkenheim, the Batdorf family of Darmstadt, the Gaukel family of Miltenberg and the Lotz family of the Palatinate.

We are direct-line descendants of soldiers who sacrificed for our freedom: Civil War servicemen Andrew G. Hensel and Daniel Updegrove, and possibly Elijah Anderson and Thomas E. Batdorf. War of 1812 servicemen Adam Frantz, Andrew W. Hensel and Joseph Workman, and possible William Row and John Gipe. Revolutionary War servicemen Andrew Messerschmidt, Andrew Miller, Frank Row, Henry Bucher, Jacob Lehman, Jacob Livezey, Jacob Philip Bordner, Jacob Rudy, John Adam Guise, John Balthaser Romberger, John Casper Hensel, John Conrad Bucher, John Daniel Angst, John Faber, John George Herrold, John George Schupp, John Henry Reiman, John Jacob Loyman John Miller, John Peter Braun (British), John Peter Shaffer, Jonas Rudy, Michael Garman, Michael Leyman, Nicholas Mantz, Peter Keefer, Valentine Welker, and William Anderson.

Our children's maternal lines include WWII servicemen Ed Mazo, Percy Forsythe and Robert Forsythe; WWI serviceman Raymond Barbush; and Civil War servicemen Cyrus Shannon, Jacob Wittle, John Shover, John Minnick, and Sebastian Shover. We are collateral descendants of Presidents Dwight D. Eisenhower and William McKinley; Pennsylvania politicians Samuel Pennypacker, John Morton, and Jonas Row; Civil War Brigadier General Galushia Penny- packer; entertainers Marlon Brando, Les Brown, and Ray W. Brown; religious leaders Conrad Weiser and Michael Enderline; and famed Melba Dodge, Jesse Runkle, Enrico Caruso, and Galla Curci. Lastly, Taylor Wittel lists relations to James Madison, Zachary Taylor, Jefferson Davis, and Gene Autry.

Our ancestors' names have been immortalized at these locations: the Bager Homestead, Abbottstown, Pennsylvania; the Chris Miller Homestead, North Lebanon Township, Pennsylvania; the Benfield homestead, Berks Co., Pennsylvania; the Livesey Homestead, Philadelphia, Pennsylvania; the Wirth Homestead, Dauphin Co., Pennsylvania; the Keefer Homestead in Berks, Pennsylvania; the Morton Homestead in Chester, Pennsylvania; the Herrold

Homestead in Northumberland, Pennsylvania; and the Jacob Lehman Homestead in Hanover, Pennsylvania. Additionally, these place names were named after our forebearers: Bordnersville, Kelly Crossroads, Livesey Street, Herrold's Island, Keefer's Station, Deibler's Gap, Deibler's Dam, and Shoemakertown, all in Pennsylvania.

The approximate percentages of relatives birthplaces are: 45% born in Pennsylvania, 17% Germany, 14% Scotland, 9% Italy, 4% Georgia, 4% South Carolina, 4% Ireland, 2% New York, and 1% Africa, Virginia, Florida, Switzerland, England, Bohemia, France, Sweden, Finland, and the West Indies.

At the moment, our paternal line breaks down to about 11/16 German, 3/16 Britain, 1/16 French, 1/16 Swiss. Our maternal line breaks down to about 10/16 German, 4/16 Britain, 1/16 French, 1/16 Swiss/Scandanavian. Our children's maternal lines break down to 7/16 Italian, 4/16 African, 2/16 Irish, 2/16 German, 1/16 West Indian/Britain.

Here are some additional interesting numerical facts for the families:

3 Ancestors who died at sea: N. Benesch, G. Reith & G. Shoemaker
3 Ancestors named Ashley or Renae
5 Number of birth states
8 Ancestors named Gerald or Gilbert
8 Most different lines with same surname: Miller, Mueller, etc.
10 Generations, FTM lines only (numerous)
11 Number of birth countries
14 Youngest age having child, female: Anna Maria Hamm & Anna Barbara Knerr
17 Youngest age having child, male, John George Werner
17 Number of children, one couple, Mary Louisa Peters/ Thomas Edward Batdorf
18 Youngest age at death, female: Emma Keefer
21 Generations, FTM & additional lines (Livesay)
22 Number of children, one man, Isabelle Penman & Mary Bast/Alexander Thompson
24 Ancestors named Sophia or Marie
24 Most letters in name, male: Howard Andrew Carson Hensel
27 Most letters in name, female: Amelia Dorothy Elizabeth Bager
30 Youngest age at death, male: William Duncan
34 Ancestors named Andrew or Roman 34 Media records, collateral lines
50 Oldest age having child, female: Veronica Schmidt
50 Most variations for single surname: Batdorf, Bodorff, Batterff, Pottorf, etc.
57 Ancestors named Connor or Adam
59.6 Average lifespan, all lines
63.2 Average lifespan, Thompson lines
68 Oldest age having child, male: Alexander Thompson
94 Oldest age at death: Sarah Faber, Anna Bleymeyer & Michael Goodman
256 Ancestors named Shirley or Mary
412 Media records, Thompson lines
491 Media records, all lines
569 Direct-line ancestors, Thompson lines
776 Place names, Thompson lines
870 Direct-line ancestors, all lines
923 Sources used, Thompson lines
983 Total surnames, Thompson line
1,328 Sources used, all lines
1,371 Place names, all lines
1,230 Total surnames, all lines
4,675 Sources checked, Thompson lines
5,801 Relatives, Thompson lines
5,825 Sources checked, all lines
8,569 Relatives, all lines
1410 Earliest birth, unrecorded lines, Geoffrey Livesay
1689 Earliest birth, recorded lines, John Wendel George Traut

This and the proceeding Family History narratives are our heritage. With this information we can be proud of ourselves and our past, and aim toward bright futures and better lives. If our duty is neglected, as each generation passes, so will our family history. We have a desire and we have a bond. We have a desire to know from whence we came. We want to know our history, our origins. We want to know what our ancestors did, how they persevered and how the spark of life made its way from Geoffrey Livesay, born over 600 years ago, to our latest cousin, born just this winter 2015.

Chapter 2:
GENERATION TWO

The history of the American Negro is the history of this strife,
He simply wishes to make it possible for a man
to be both a Negro and an American...
- W.E.B. Du Bois

A family is like a forest, when you are outside it is dense,
when you are inside you see that each tree has its place.
- African Proverb

Our parents are including in the second generation, comprising those born in from about 1910 to 1950. Those living are not included in this book, so this is the only narrative for this family included in this book.

Our Curry and Mazo (originally Mason) families were located in the deep South, part of Georgia and South Carolina. We are indebted to their struggles and pain, and the ultimate triumph to bring us freedom and opportunity.

Eddie Mazo & Dolores A. Curry

The baby boy who would become Eddie Mazo was born to Mack Mason and Sarah Thompson of Jefferson County, Georgia, on September 7, 1912. Edward was born their fifth child, joining a family that already included two older brothers and two older sisters, Jesse, John, Annie Lee, and Maria. After Edward's birth, siblings Mack, Robert, and Melvin were born to the Masons.

Mack and Sarah Mason named their son Edward Mason after Mack's father, Edward "Ned" Mason. The senior Edward held a special position in the family based on the fact that he represented the last generation of this Mason family to be born a slave. He had had been freed as a young man by Abraham Lincoln's Emancipation Proclamation and guaranteed equality of rights by the 13th, 14th, and 15th Amendments to the U.S. Constitution.

Unfortunately, as soon as Georgia was readmitted to the Union in 1871—the last previously Confederate state to be accepted—Federal troops started pulling out. With the direct threat reduced, former Confederates and their offspring began trying every political trick they could to keep the black Georgians from achieving equality with the whites. By 1916, every black person in Georgia had come to understand the wide gap between what the Federal Government promised and what the state and local governments delivered. Just before Edward Mason's birth, the State of Georgia had gone so far as to issue an official State charter for the rebirth of the Ku Klux Klan, which had been closed down and wiped out by the Federal troops.

To be sure, black people were organizing and working for change—more than a million and a half left the south and moved to the industrial cities of the northeast and mid-west. The NAACP had been formed in New York in 1909, and was heavily pushing court cases to end lynching and overturn the Jim Crow laws that legalized racial segregation. They were having some successes, but progress was slow and the families that stayed in Georgia still had lives to live as best they could.

Mack Mason worked hard to provide for his family, sometimes as a farm laborer or a stable hand, and sometimes as a sharecropper farmer. But even for a hard-working man, jobs were not always available for a laborer in rural Georgia. Mack and his family often had to follow opportunity from place to place. When Edward Mason was born, Mack was working as a day laborer at a saw mill in Louisville, Georgia. Day laborers only work when there is a need for them—there was no assurance of working every day.

Circumstances following Edward's birth suggest that Sarah may have had a hard time with the birth, or may have suffered an illness afterwards. As already mentioned Edward was his mother's fifth child in nine years. The strain of so many children, combined with having to shift house and worry about money, may have been too heavy a load. Whatever the reason, the family apparently needed some relief—and the solution that they found would change Edward's life forever. They decided to send Edward to live with his Aunt Ida in her home in Atlanta, Georgia.

When Edward Mason came to her, Ida Jones, a recent widow, was a clothing presser for a department store. She was also already acting as a temporary surrogate mother for a niece named Jeraline Banks. Ida shared a house with three other adult women. Two of them worked outside the house, but one lady stayed at home and made her money by taking in laundry. Also, Jeraline was eleven years old when Edward came so she could act as playmate and sometimes as babysitter for him. She could always call the older woman for help if she needed it. This allowed Ida to work without worrying too much about having an adult close at hand if needed.

The arrangement between Mack and Sarah Mason and Aunt Ida was probably intended to be a temporary one—just a break meant to give Edward's folks a little rest and some breathing room. But month ran into month, and then year ran into year, and it turned out that Edward Mason lived with his Aunt Ida until he was fifteen years old. By then, Ida was referring to him as her son. During these years with Aunt Ida, Edward got most of his schooling, made friends, and first started noticing girls. It was also during these years with Ida that Edward met a man named Mazo, a war hero, who family stories say made a great impression on young Edward and whom he came to greatly admire. Motivated by this admiration—and maybe also by some resentment towards a family that he felt had abandoned him—Edward took it on himself to change his name to Eddie Mazo.

By 1930, the times in Georgia and America had changed—and not for the better. The Jim Crow problems and the Great Depression had roared in, making life much tougher than it had been. Bread lines popped up around Atlanta, and men who had worked all their lives found themselves hoping for a handout. Like tens of thousands of other people, Aunt Ida—who was also getting older—lost her job with the department store. Her younger brother, Wallis Oliver, a recent widower, came to live with them. He, at least, was still working—also as a clothing presser. But even for people who still had jobs, wages were low, money was scarce, and living was difficult.

In April of that year, perhaps to alleviate some of the hardship on Ida, Eddie left his Aunt's house and went to live with the family of Jeraline Banks in Birmingham, Alabama. Henry Banks, Jeraline's father, and Gary Smith, Jeraline's new husband, still had jobs with a freight company. They loaded and unloaded trucks and worked in the warehouse.

The Banks family took Eddie in and called him their adopted son. Since Eddie worked in similar industries for much of his later life, it is likely they also got Eddie at least part-time work with them at some point. But one thing did not change. When the census taker came to the house that year, Eddie was listed as Edward Mazo. And that is how he always introduced himself.

Even though he never lived with his parents, it is likely that Eddie had at least occasional contact with some of his family. When he was in his early twenties, he moved to Savannah, Georgia, where most of the Masons were living at the time. He found a job there working with trucks for the State of Georgia. A few years later, he changed his job direction and found work as a cook.

In Savannah, Edward met and married a woman named Florence, and they soon had a daughter named Constance. The marriage very quickly appeared to be in trouble and continued up and down for some years. In November of 1945, with World War II all but over, the U.S. Army was still recruiting men for the huge job of bringing the boys home and returning U.S. installations to peacetime mode. Eddie enlisted in the Army Air Corps and spent nearly two years in Hawaii. It seems likely that at least part of his motivation was the chance to get away from his troubled marriage.

After he came home from the military, Eddie reunited briefly with Florence, but by the mid-fifties, the marriage was over. Eddie also had a daughter named Sarah with another woman, and he continued to live in Savannah, Georgia, for most of the remainder of his life. It is here in Savannah where Eddie would meet Delores Ann Curry.

Delores was born on February 24, 1948, in Savannah, Georgia, the child of Robert Joseph Forsyth and Cressie Jo Curry. Both of Delores's parents were also natives of Savannah, and Delores grew up and went to school there.

When Delores was in her late teens, she met Eddie and they had a daughter, Melvalean Curry, and a son, both born in the 1960s. Eddie was often not home and Delores had to raise the children with bare necessities. Opportunities for a single black woman with a family in the South were nearly nonexistent. Racism was still rampant and economic viability was low. Delores left Eddie shortly thereafter, moving to Philadelphia, Pennsylvania, and remarrying. She lived out her life in Philadelphia, and died there on December 16, 2000, at the age of 52.

In his last few years, Eddie had moved to Plains, Georgia, where he died on December 20, 1997. Eddie's World War II service in the Army Air Corps earned him the right of burial in a National Cemetery, and he was buried with honors in Section I, Row 682, of the Andersonville National Historic Site in Macon County, Georgia. This famous cemetery began during the Civil War as the final resting place for Union soldiers who perished while POWs at the nearby Confederate Camp Sumter, better known as Andersonville Prison Camp. Eddie and Delores's daughter, Melvalean Curry Thompson, is the family's direct ancestor.

Chapter 3:
GENERATION THREE

The four grandparents Sarah and Mack Mason and Cressie Jo and Robert J. W. Forsyth comprise the Third Generation and is the starting point for the detailed biographies included in this volume. Their birth dates ranges from late 1800s to the early 1900s. To place them in understandable location and time, the following information was downloaded from our ancestry.com FTM file. This brief biographical information, and the historical text that follows, will allow the reader to not only identify the starting point of the following biographies, but also allow a better understanding of the times, places and events.

The Ford Model T of 1908 was the first automobile mass produced on assembly lines with completely interchangeable parts. It was the automobile that opened up travel to the common middle-class. The innovation of the assembly line was revolutionary.

World War I, beginning in 1914, was a conflict involving most of the world's powers. The beginning of the war was sparked by the assassination of Archduke Franz Ferdinand of Austria Hungary. The world quickly formed into alliances, The Allied Powers—United Kingdom, France, The Russian Empire, and later the United States—fought against the Central Powers—The German Empire, The Austro-Hungarian Empire, The Ottoman Empire and the Kingdom of Bulgaria. Over 70 million military personnel fought in the war including 60 million Europeans. The Western Front consisted of a trench line that changed little until 1917. More than 15 million people were killed; making World War I one of the deadliest conflicts in history.

The Great Depression was a worldwide economic downturn that started with the stock market crash of 1929. The depression varied in countries around the world but generally started in 1929 and lasted until the beginning of World War II. Unemployment rose to 25% in the US and as high as 33% in other countries. Countries whose jobs primarily came from industry suffered the most. The Great Depression was the largest economic downturn in history.

The Holocaust refers to the systematic genocide of over six million European Jews by Nazi Germany. The genocide began in stages in the early 1930's by removing Jews from society; moving the Jews to concentration camps, where they died of slave labor and disease; moving Jews to ghettos; mass shootings in conquered territories; and finally extermination camps where most Jews who survived the journey were killed in gas chambers.

World War II began on September 1, 1939 with the German invasion of Poland. The war involved most of the world's powers and was divided into two sides: the Allies versus the Axis. World War II changed the boundaries of war with significant actions against civilians including the Holocaust and the only use of nuclear weapons in war. 100 million military personnel were involved in the conflict. World War II was the deadliest war in history with over 70 million casualties. World War II ended in 1945 with the victory of The Allies.

Mack Mason & Sarah A. Thompson

The morning of September 25, 1880, came into Washington County, Georgia, cool and clear, with wide blue skies and light breezes. "Shirt-sleeve weather," the locals called it. It was so like all the other late September days in that part of Georgia it was only made memorable for Edward "Ned" Mason and his wife, Ranie, by the arrival of their newest son, Mack Mason.

Ned and Ranie had married young, and children had followed quickly and regularly, so that even though Ned and Ranie were only 33 and 27, respectively, Mack was their seventh child and their fifth son. Waiting to meet the new baby boy were older brothers George, Jim, Plum, and Austin, and sisters Jane and Dicey. And Mack would not be Ned and Ranie's last child—he would himself become older brother to two brothers, Alonzo and Oliver, and two sisters, Janice and Ella. Ned Mason and Ranie Brown had been born as slaves on the plantations of Washington County, Georgia. They had been freed by the Civil War and the Emancipation Proclamation. Mack and his brothers and sisters were the first generation to be born free.

As a slave, Mack Mason's father had been a farmhand and he continued to do that work for wages as a free man. But times were hard and pay was poor—everyone had to do what they could to help the family. This meant that education often took a backseat to financial need, and Mack only got through the fifth grade before he went to help, as had each of his brothers in their turn.

Mack Mason was born into a strange time in the lives of Georgia's freed slaves. For almost twenty years, African Americans in Georgia had been enjoying relatively mild political and racial relations with their white neighbors—which is what they had hoped for when emancipation had come.

To be sure, this favorable climate did not spring from good will on the part of former slave owners and Confederates who had started the Civil War in an effort to keep their slaves. Indeed, as soon as possible after the close of the Civil War, the former slave owners and Confederate veterans had regained control of the Georgia Legislature. They had then immediately passed harsh laws intended to remove the black man's recently granted right to vote and to physically and socially segregate black and white Georgians.

The U.S. Congress, though, totally controlled by Union men and in no mood to tolerate bad acts by former Confederates, brought out the hobnailed boots and kicked the white supremacists' plans to pieces. A series of new Federal laws intended to suppress the white supremacists' actions forced the former Confederates to backpedal. As a result, nearly all of the recently passed racist laws in the eleven former Confederate states were repealed by 1868. In addition, the 13th, 14th, and 15th

Amendments to the U.S. Constitution were ratified with the intent of guaranteeing the former slaves and their descendants all of the rights due the white majority.

The effect of the Congressional actions was strong and immediate. Between 1867 and 1872, sixty-nine African Americans served as delegates to the Georgia State Constitutional Convention or as members of the Georgia State Legislature. Jefferson Franklin Long, a tailor from Bibb County, sat in the U.S. Congress from December 1870 to March 1871. Former slaves and slave owners shopped in the same stores, used the same banks, and walked on the same sidewalks.

With all of this forced change, Georgia was still a potentially dangerous place for the African American. A wrong word or even a particular glance at the wrong place or time could easily get a black man killed. Between 1880 and 1930, more than 450 men were lynched in Georgia, and prosecutions for those killings were rare.

But the years of Mack Mason's early childhood were times when, if they were a little careful, former slaves and their children could begin to feel, if not the full winds, surely the breezes of freedom. Mack, as a young boy going out to work, had little reason to suspect that, by his sixteenth birthday, events would create a very strong turn for the worse.

Having the Federal Government slap them down did not alter the segregationists' goal one iota. They still tested the waters on a regular basis by passing segregationist laws where they thought they might get away with it. In early

1872, Georgia schools were segregated. Then some cities and towns began mandating separate black and white cemeteries. But the real troubles began in 1883, when the U.S. Supreme Court ruled that, while the Federal Government could govern discrimination by other governmental bodies, the Constitution gave it no power over discrimination by individual citizens.

Former slave states saw this as a signal to start trying to expand the envelope on segregation. New restrictive laws were passed in the different states and some survived. Then in 1890, Louisiana passed a law requiring that railroads provide separate cars for blacks and whites. Determined to fight the law, a concerned group of prominent black, Creole, and white residents of New Orleans formed a Committee of Citizens with the stated purpose of attempting to repeal the law. The best thing, they decided, would be to create a case that would test the law in the courts. In 1892, one of the group—a mixed race man named Homer Plessy—bought a first-class ticket, boarded a "whites only" car, and found himself a seat. Mr. Plessy was immediately asked to move to the "blacks only" car, which he refused to do. He was arrested on the spot and the Committee of Citizens had their case.

The case, which was known as *Plessy vs Ferguson,* spent the next four years winding its way through the local and state courts. Finally, in 1896, it came before the United States Supreme Court. As the Court convened for oral arguments on April

13, 1896, there was little to suggest that the ultimate outcome of *Plessy vs Ferguson* was going to be far worse for African Americans than anyone could have imagined.

Simply stated, the majority of the Supreme Court ruled that there was nothing in the Constitution, including the new 13th, 14th, and 15th Amendments, that prohibited the forced separation of the black and white races in public facilities. The Constitution, according to the Court, required that all citizens be protected equally, but that as long as the separate facilities provided to African Americans were equal to those provided to whites, no inherent violation of the U.S. Constitution would occur.

As each of the governments of the former slave states immediately perceived, the *Plessy* decision essentially legitimized the state laws establishing racial segregation in the South. All the various states had to do to totally exclude their black citizens from public places was to claim that separate and equal facilities had been provided for them. For the next sixty years, "Separate but Equal" would be the catchphrase that white supremacists would use to repress and separate black people from the mainstream white society.

But in 1896, the average American—black or white—did not typically follow the workings of the Supreme Court, and few of them saw what was on the horizon. Oblivious to exactly what was coming, Mack Mason, went on with the process of shifting from boyhood to being a man.

Mack was a fully grown young man out of his parent's house and living on his own when he met and courted a pretty nineteen-year-old named Sarah Shatteen Thompson, commonly called Sallie. His courtship was ultimately successful, and Mack and Sallie were married on December 15, 1902, in Washington County, Georgia.

Sallie Thompson had been born in June of 1883 in Washington County, Georgia, to parents Peter Thompson and Ann M. Shatteen. Sadly, Sallie's mother died when she was only five years old. Sallie's father had to work, so she went to live with her grandmother, Sallie Shatteen, for whom she was named. She was still living with her grandmother when she married Mack Mason.

By the time of their marriage, many of the harsh segregation laws that the white supremacists had been pushing had been put in place. The collection of repressive laws that forced separation between whites and African Americans in nearly every element of life became known as "Jim Crow." The name was taken from a character in a mid-1800s minstrel show in which white men would dress up in blackface and outlandish costumes and sing and dance to "colored" music. History does not record when or how the name became associated with the pattern of segregationist laws, but everyone soon knew what it meant.

And what Jim Crow meant for black people was all bad. By 1910, ten of the eleven former Confederate states had passed new constitutions or amendments to existing constitutions that used a combination of poll taxes, literacy and comprehension tests, along with residency and record-keeping requirements, to effectively disenfranchise most blacks and tens of thousands of poor whites. Suddenly, black men who had been voting for nearly 30 years were suddenly told that they were no longer qualified to vote.

The deliberate and unapologetic nature of these acts is shown by a law passed in Oklahoma. Seeing that their new anti-black laws were also causing thousands of poor whites to lose their voting rights, Oklahoma passed an incredibly cynical amendment to their new law stating that anyone who had voted, or whose ancestor had voted, prior to 1866, would be exempt from the restrictive elements of the new law. Since only white men voted prior to 1866, this amendment made all white men exempt from the literacy test and the other new requirements.

In Washington, D.C., Woodrow Wilson, the first Southern-born President since the Civil War, had apparently decided to become the "Racist-in-Chief." The Federal Government had been integrated pretty much since the Civil War. Wilson changed that by firing all black department heads, demoting a number of black military officers to noncommissioned officers, and, where black employees were not fired, segregating departments into black and white offices.

In the various states, all public facilities were suddenly made separate. From the iconic water fountains, to buses, street cars, restaurants, bathrooms, city and county parks, doctor's offices, and on and on, henceforth, some were for blacks, some for whites—none were for both.

Blacks and whites could not marry, could not share hospital rooms, could not play baseball together, could not be in the same insane asylums, and could not be buried in the same cemeteries. The goal seemed to be to make the black people invisible to white society—and it seemed to be working. The progress made during the years since the Civil War had been turned on its head. Anyone violating one of these laws could easily end up in jail . . . or worse. This was the world in which Mack and Sallie Mason began their married lives.

Mack Mason was a hard-working man who did what was necessary to provide for his family. While growing up, his only training had been in farm labor, and early in his marriage he usually worked as a farmhand. Farm work often came and went with the season, requiring the family to sometimes move to follow the work. In the years after their marriage, Mack, Sallie, and the family moved to Louisville, Jefferson County, Georgia, where they lived for many years.

Mack worked as a stable hand on a farm for a while, and then later worked at a sawmill in the same area. After the sawmill work ended, Mack got a chance to farm for himself as a sharecropper. The farm was in Wadley, Jefferson County, Georgia, and he rented it by agreeing to share the profits of the crops that he raised. It was during these years in Washington and Jefferson Counties that Mack and Sallie's seven children were born: Jesse, John, Annie Lee, Maria, Eddie, Robert, and Melvin. Eddie—the progenitor of this line—would eventually honor his brother, Melvin, using his name as the base for his daughter's name, Melvalean.

Sometime between Melvin Mason's birth and April of 1930, Mack and Sallie moved the family to Savannah, Georgia, where Mack and Sallie lived out the remainder of their lives. Mack worked for some years in a fertilizer plant, and later got a job as a woodcutter in a pulpwood mill. It would be the job that he finally retired from.

Sallie Thompson Mason, a dedicated wife, mother, and support for her husband, came down with cancer and succumbed to it in Savannah on March 21, 1938. She and Mack had been married for 35 years. Sallie was buried in the Lincoln Cemetery, Chatham County, Georgia. Mack lived on in Savannah for another 24 years. He never remarried. He retired in the early 1940s, and lived with his daughter Annie Lee after that. Mack died in her house on September 18, 1962.

Mack had been born during the relatively brief period following the Civil War when it appeared that African Americans in Georgia were going get at least most of the rights guaranteed them by the U.S. Constitution. He went on to live the bulk of his life under the heavy weight of the Jim Crow laws that stole that promise away from them. But before he died, he got to see the beginnings of change: the rise of leaders like Martin Luther King and the passage of the first laws that would start the pendulum swinging back toward a greater freedom again.

Mack and Sallie's fifth child, Eddie Mason, is the direct ancestor of this family line. Eddie was born at a hard time for Sallie and the family. As a result, he spent most of his life being raised by willing relatives. During this period, he met an Army man named Mazo whom he came to greatly admire. [See the previous narrative fore details]

Robert J. W. Forsyth & Cressie Jo Curry

Wednesday, the fifteenth of September, 1926—the day that Robert Joseph Washington Forsyth was born as the second child of Percy Campbell Forsythe and Nina Washington—dawned hot and muggy in the city of Savannah, Georgia. Despite the fact that the first day of fall was only nine days away, summer was tenaciously refusing to surrender its hold, and the citizens of the city had resigned themselves to another day of sweating in the sweltering heat. To Robert, of course, it made little difference. It was his day and his time.

Unfortunately, it was a difficult time in Georgia. Soaring manufacturing and production were making the early 1920s boom times for much of America, but not for all. In the South, and especially in Georgia, earlier economic good times had been built on the back of a strong cotton industry. And by the time that Robert J. was born, overproduction, foreign competition, new man-made fabrics, a long drought—and worst of all, the boll-weevil—had seriously devastated Georgia's cotton-based economy.

Then in October of 1929, when Robert J. was only three years old, the financial collapse that became known as the Great Depression began and times got very hard for the entire world. Life was especially harsh for blacks, many of whom were part of Georgia's sharecropping farming culture. Unable to earn a living, many were forced off their land entirely by declining crop prices. Some took to the road, heading north into major urban areas and industrial centers. But many found themselves forced into Georgia's towns and cities, where they often competed with locals for menial jobs.

Fortunately, Savannah, as one of America's premier seaports, fared better than most of Georgia. Some businesses, such as the paper pulp and food- and sugar-processing industries that had begun prior to the Depression, were able to not only survive, but to thrive. No working man was going to get rich, but there were jobs to be had. This was the environment in which Robert J. Forsythe spent his first fifteen years

Robert's father, Percy, was one of those men who benefited from the Port of Savannah. He worked as a cook on a steamship of the Steamship of Savannah Company that hauled cargo and passengers from the Port of New York to Boston and then on to Savannah, Georgia. The ship then made the same trip in reverse with a new cargo and passenger load. The job was steady, and it probably paid better than many jobs that were available locally. But it was also a job that often left Nina and Robert at home alone for weeks at a time.

Savannah's port facilities also played a prominent role in World War II. When the war that would soon become World War II started in Europe in 1939, the U.S. started sending supplies overseas to help England. To help do this, they contracted ships belonging to the Savannah Steamship Company. Beginning in September 1941, Percy Forsythe's ship ended passenger service began carrying only cargoes considered important to the U.S. war effort. At the same time, the shipyard at the Port of Savannah began gearing up and was soon one of the nation's most active Atlantic shipyards for the construction of Liberty Ship transports for the U.S. war effort.

At nine minutes after nine, on the evening of 19 January, 1942, Percy Forsythe's ship, the *City of Atlanta,* was about eight miles off Cape Hatteras, North Carolina, en route to Savannah, when it was torpedoed by a German submarine. The ship was badly damaged and quickly rolled over and sank before any lifeboats could be launched. Percy and forty-two other sailors died in the attack.

The death of his father at the hands of the German submarine seems to have had a major and very specific effect on sixteen year-old Robert J. Forsythe: ten months later, Robert went to the U.S. Navy recruiting station and enlisted. He almost certainly had to lie about his age to do so.

Because of his race and his age, Robert was assigned to the Messman Branch of the Navy—which was soon retitled as the Steward Branch. At the beginning of 1942, whites were not allowed to serve in the Steward Branch, and the entire Branch was made up of black and Filipino sailors. The Steward Branch was responsible for feeding everyone on the ship, but after Robert's training and satisfaction of a required period of service, he was rated as a Stewards Mate 1st Class. Men in this specialty were essentially waiters for the officer's mess (dining room).

This should not be taken to mean that Robert had no other duties or that he never faced the dangers of war. Stewards were actually the first African Americans to see action in World War II because following Pearl Harbor the Navy was more or less in regular contact with the enemy. And every man on a ship had a battle station when the action started. Indeed, it was after several Stewards had been recognized for extreme bravery in battle that the Navy realized that it was missing a bet and dropped its ban on African Americans serving in fields outside the Steward Branch.

Following three years of service in World War II, Robert was discharged on 15 November, 1945. Undoubtedly, he, like most African Americans returning from the war, hoped to find that his service would warrant better treatment than he had experienced growing up. If so, he was destined to be disappointed.

Racially, Savannah had always had something of split personality. During the early days of slavery, the white population had shown an unusually liberal disposition toward slaves. Slaves had been allowed to have their own public church, which could be attended by slaves from all over the city—something unheard in other slave states. After the abolition of slavery, white Savannah prided itself on having a more "genteel" relationship with the black population. In truth, Savannah never had the same level of violence between blacks and whites that was found in other Georgia cities. And certainly, as the war ended in the 1940s, Savannah's business leaders wanted to show a more cosmopolitan face to the growing numbers of foreign tourists that had begun coming into America through her port. They wanted the world believe in the idea of the city's genteel view of race relations.

But while less violent and less obvious than other Georgia cities, Jim Crow still lived in Savannah's streets. Returning black servicemen often found themselves either denied the right to vote outright, or having so many roadblocks placed in their paths it amounted to the same thing. They still had to use separate facilities from whites. Black schools still had insufficient resources, and in most places blacks were still forced to sit in the back of the bus. It was a bitter disappointment; but a man had to live and had to work to do so, and Robert Forsythe got on with it as best he could.

It was during this period of readjustment that Robert met a young woman named Lucretia "Cressie" Jo Curry, and romance ensued. Cressie Jo was also a native of Savannah, having been born there on March 5, 1929, as the first child of Frederick Curry and his young wife, Elizabeth Brown.

Despite being their first child, little Cressie Jo always found herself surrounded by numerous older children. Her father, a hardworking and responsible man, had taken the responsibility for looking after all seven of his new wife's minor siblings when both of her parents died suddenly and unexpectedly.

Frederick Curry supported this crowd, along with his own increasing family, by working as a laborer in a fertilizer plant and later as a "blocker" for a shipping company, where he ran a cotton compressor—a machine for compacting the large raw cotton bales into smaller, rectangular sizes to allow more of them to fit into the available space on a cargo ship.

As each of Elizabeth Brown Curry's siblings got older, they moved out on their own or to live with one another. But while the aunts and uncles were growing up and moving out, the Curry family was having children of their own. By the time Cressie Jo was ten years old, all of the Browns were out of the house, and they had been replaced by her own sister, Nancy, and her brothers, Frederick, Jr., Frank, and Sam.

Cressie Jo was in her late teens when she met Robert Forsythe, and was only nineteen years old when they married in Savannah, Georgia, on April 17, 1948. Robert Forsythe was twenty-one years old. Robert and Cressie Jo's daughter, Delores Ann Curry, was born that same year.

As it turned out, Robert and Cressie Jo's marriage was rather short-lived. Robert had a hard time adjusting back into the City he had left as a teenager, and had encountered some hard times following his term in the Navy. And he had apparently fallen in with some reckless friends.

In January of 1949, less than a year after his marriage to Cressie Jo, Robert Forsythe was arrested and convicted of five counts of burglary. He was sentenced to spend a minimum of five years and a maximum of twenty years in the State penitentiary, and on February 9, 1949, he entered prison. It no doubt broke Cressie Jo's heart, but the long prison term also quickly resulted in the termination of Robert and Cressie Jo's brief marriage.

Shortly after the dissolution of her marriage to Robert Forsythe, Cressie Jo had children with Edward Mazo, her future son-in-law. It was an on-again, off-again relationship, with Edward and Cressie Jo living together, parting, and coming together again for several years before parting yet again.

Over the years, Cressie Jo and Edward Mazo had several children, including four daughters: Eddie Mae, Rainey, Gobbie Denise, and Selena; and five sons: Kenneth, James, Mark, Emmanuel, and Eddie. All were born in Savannah, Georgia.

In the end, Edward Mazo finally left for good. This time, Cressie Jo's older sons were of an age to get work and help support the family, and she never remarried. Life in Savannah got better for African Americans: civil rights laws were passed by Congress and locally a very strong and effective civil rights movement was proving successful at moving local laws and attitudes in a better direction.

Cressie Jo spent most of her life in Savannah, Georgia, raising her children and watching them begin their own families. In 1965, she went to Philadelphia,

Pennsylvania, where she had relatives, and lived there for about a year before returning to Savannah. In her last years—when her children were all grown and gone— Cressie Jo went to live with her son Kenneth in Hinesville, Georgia.

On December 10, 1998, Cressie Jo died in the Liberty Regional Medical Center in Hinesville, Liberty County, Georgia. She was buried in the Midway Congregational Church Cemetery in Hinesville.

As for Robert Forsythe, when he was released from prison he left Georgia permanently, seeking an opportunity for a new life. Apparently, he found that opportunity in Seattle, Washington, where he settled and lived out the remainder of his life. Robert Forsythe died there on November 22, 1999, and was buried in the Tahoma National Cemetery in Kent, King County, Washington, with military honors, in recognition of his World War II service. Cressie Jo Curry and Robert Forsythe's child, Delores Curry, is the direct ancestor of this family line.

Chapter 4:
GENERATION FOUR

Our Fourth Generation includes Edward and Ranie Mason, Anne and Peter Thompson, Nina and Robert Forsyth and Elizabeth and Frederick Curry of the mid to late 1800s in Georgia, South Carolina and Nassau, Bahamas.

Edward Mason & Ranie Brown

Edward "Ned" Mason was born into slavery on a plantation in Washington County, Georgia, in the year 1847. He was the first child of the young couple Alfred and Hannah Mason, who had both been born into slavery themselves, probably on the same plantation where Edward was born.

Unless Edward was born during the night, Alfred would not have met his new son until he returned to his quarters after finishing his day's work. But female slaves were typically given two or three days off after childbirth, so Hannah would have had little time to welcome Edward into his new world.

Edward was followed the next year his by the birth of his brother Noah. A five-year break between the birth of Noah and the next son, Thomas, in 1853, suggests the likelihood that Alfred and Hannah lost a child or two to stillbirth or death in early childhood. But after Thomas, Edward got a new brother or sister every year or two for the next seventeen years. There was his brother James, sister Linda, brothers Andrew, Jacob, George, and Jefferson, sister Josephine, brother Alfred, and lastly, brother Cleveland, born in 1870.

As mentioned earlier, Edward and his family were part of a Washington County, Georgia, plantation. But hearing of a "plantation," we should not be too quick to visualize the estates of white-columned mansions surrounded by miles of cotton fields that were presented to us in films such as *Gone With the Wind.* According to the 1850 U.S. Census, 1,342 white families lived in Washington County that year. An addendum to that census, known as the Slave Schedule, reported that 607 of those families—46% of the white families—owned a total of 5,809 slaves. This gave Washington County a much higher rate of slave ownership than the average for the state as a whole, at 37%. There were, however, very few of the movie-style grand plantations with their hundreds of slaves. Several plantations did hold 80 or more slaves, but the average slaveholder owned between one and eight slaves. It is far more likely, therefore, that the plantation on which the Masons lived and worked was more like a large working farm.

Customs and requirements for slave behavior and treatment varied from plantation to plantation, but in Georgia many slaves were able to live in family units, spending their limited time away from the masters' fields together. Georgia slave families also frequently cultivated their own gardens, and some were even allowed to raise livestock or supplement their families' diets by hunting and fishing. Some were permitted to gather wild berries during their off-time and sell them for money, which they were allowed to keep. They were typically given Sundays off to pursue these activities. There was a payoff to the slave owner too, of course—in the form of reduced costs for feeding his slaves.

Eventually, Christianity came to serve as a pillar of slave life in Georgia. Unlike their masters, slaves drew from Christianity the message of black equality and empowerment. In the early nineteenth century, African American preachers played a significant role in spreading the Gospel in the quarters.

Regardless of the liberalness or harshness of plantation culture, one thing was pretty much constant on each plantation: every slave there was expected to work. As a very small child, Edward would have had a relatively simple life. He would have been tended to by one of older children—if there were any—or maybe by an elderly slave woman who could no longer do her usual work. The small children would have been free to play and sleep.

However, by the time Edward was seven or eight, he would have been assigned tasks that he could be expected to complete, such as pulling weeds around the house or walking down the rows of tobacco plants picking caterpillars off the leaves and stalks. When he was a couple of years older, he might have been put to churning butter and fetching eggs from the chicken pens. Unless he got assigned to a particular job, such as caring for the animals, this progression toward heavier work would have continued until his middle to late teens, when he would have gone to the fields with the other men.

Edward Mason was sixteen years old when Abraham Lincoln's Emancipation Proclamation went into effect in January of 1863. Legally, he was free as of that moment, and with so many of the white slave masters away in the Civil War, some slaves did take the chance and begin to slip away looking for opportunities to make it on their own. Most blacks, however, remained enslaved for another year or more until Sherman's march to the sea reached its goal in Savannah and the Union Army was able to put some teeth into the Proclamation. Edward was eighteen when the Civil War ended in 1865, and slavery finally collapsed everywhere across the Confederacy. He was finally and forever free—though there were times during the coming years when it may not have felt like such a great gift.

Jobs were scarce and times were hard in those first years. Much of Georgia's wealth had been destroyed by the war and the collapse of slavery. Most of the former slave owners still had land, but without their slaves, making it profitable again was difficult. This often made life hard for both the former slave owner and former slave alike. The lack of jobs and the fear of starvation made it fairly common in those first hard years for freedmen to go back to their old plantations and work the same fields they had worked as slaves.

But there were major differences now. From the end of the Civil War until 1877, the State of Georgia was under the control of the U.S. military. Troops and Union officials overseeing the civilian leadership ensured that the new laws guaranteeing the rights of the freedmen were not violated—or that they were violated less frequently. The military also set up a court of sorts where disputes between blacks and whites could be settled fairly. These courts had arrest powers, and they also dealt swiftly with any violence or retaliation done to the freedmen by their former owners.

For the first time in his life, Edward Mason had a choice as to what he would do with his life. Under the circumstances, he initially elected to continue to work at what he knew, so he went back to the fields. But now it was his choice, and he worked as a hired hand for wages. The wages were small in those first days, but he also found that his time was now his own, and when he was not working he got to decide how to spend it. And on the third day of July in 1867, Edward spent his time doing something that neither he nor anyone else had ever thought that he would be able to do. He registered as an eligible voter in Washington County, Georgia. For the remainder of his life, Edward would be one of the deciders of how he would be governed.

At about the same time he became a voter, Edward Mason met a young neighbor girl named Ranie Brown, a freed slave like himself. Edward went on to court Ranie, and the two were married about 1869. Ranie was only eighteen when she married Edward Mason.

Ranie Brown had been born in Washington County, Georgia, in December of 1852. She was the first child of George and Mary A. Brown. Ranie's father, George, had become a sharecropper farmer within a few years of the collapse of slavery, and he and Mary built a life on the farm. Ranie was their first daughter, but she was soon joined by his sisters Rachel and Mary, and brothers Samuel, Simon, and Remus.

Ranie was barely thirteen when slavery ended, and her life on the plantation would have been very different from Edward's simply because she was freed before she became old enough for the heavy field or house work. That does not, of course, mean that she got away with not working. Like the boys, the girls were assigned tasks as soon as they were deemed old enough to perform them. Ranie would have been old enough to watch the younger children, help clean the slave master's house, churn butter, or help pick pests off the crops. Her heaviest work came later when she married Edward Mason and became the mother of twelve children.

Edward worked hard and was soon able to get his own farm on a sharecropping contract. There, his and Ranie's own family grew quickly. Their first son, George W. Brown, was born by the end of their first year of marriage, and over the next eighteen years they had ten additional children: James Mason in 1872, Aggie in 1872, Jane in 1875, Dicey in 1876, Austin in 1878, Mack in 1880, Alonzo in 1882, Janice in 1885, Ella in 1886, and Oliver in 1888.

Sometime between 1888 and 1900, Edward "Ned" Mason died in Washington County, Georgia. Some might think him lucky—he had lived to see the ending of slavery in America, he had managed his own business for his own benefit and that of his children, and he had expressed his opinion on how he should be governed through his vote. And in the end, his journey ended before the tragedy of the Jim Crow era began.

After Edward's death, Ranie Brown Mason lived on in Washington County with her children. And Ranie did live long enough to see the beginning of the Jim Crow era bring a major erosion of the freedoms won by Civil War and Emancipation. She had to watch as stores, banks, and other businesses went from being open to everyone to being for whites only. Ranie had to watch the black man lose the right to vote after forty years of voting. And she had to watch her sons walk carefully around white women, where a simple glance taken wrong could end in a lynching. It wasn't as bad as slavery, but it no longer really felt like freedom, either.

Ranie Brown Mason died in Washington County, Georgia, sometime between 1910 and 1920. Edward and Ranie's son, Mack Mason, became the direct ancestor of this family line.

Peter Thompson & Anne M. Shatteen

February of 1860 was cold in Jefferson County, Georgia, especially in the slave quarters where fires were used only on the coldest nights. It was not a particularly good place or time to be born, but here he was anyway, Peter Thompson—first and only child of his father and Polly Thompson—taking his first breath. The women who helped with the birth had gone to their cabins or to work, and her husband had also just been called to work, as usual. Polly, though, had been allowed a few days lying-in time to get the baby off to a good start. She hugged the baby to her chest and tucked the blanket in around them as best she could. As she drifted back to sleep, she wondered briefly what life would have in store for her son. But not in her wildest dreams could she have imagined the turbulent times into which he had just been born.

Totally unknown to the Thompsons, within days of Peter's birth, Illinois lawyer and politician Abraham Lincoln would make a speech in New York City at a private college called The Cooper Union. His goal was to introduce himself to New York as a candidate for Republican nomination for President of the United States. He spoke of his opposition to slavery and to its spread into new territories and states that would be created from America's expansion into the West.

The speech would achieve his goal beyond all expectations. The *New York Times* and the *New York Tribune* both published the speech, and the *Tribune* hailed it as "one of the happiest and most convincing political arguments ever made in this City . . . No man ever made such an impression on his first appeal to a New-York audience." To top it off, just prior to the speech Lincoln had visited the photography shop of Matthew Brady and sat for a few photos. Four days after the speech, one of these photographs of Lincoln appeared on the cover of *Harper's Weekly* magazine.

Two months later, Lincoln won the nomination as the Republican candidate for President, and six months after that he was elected President of the United States. Lincoln later remarked that Matthew Brady and his day at The Cooper Union had made him President.

Back in Georgia, slaves on the plantations had still heard almost nothing about Lincoln. But soon the talk among the whites was about little else than Lincoln and his enmity towards slavery. Indeed, prior to the election, several of the slave states had vowed to secede if he was elected. By the time of Peter Thompson's first birthday, slave owners across the South were in an uproar, and nearly every slave had heard of Abraham Lincoln. Seven states, including Georgia, had seceded from the United States, and four more would soon follow.

Surviving records show that Georgia originally hoped for a peaceful and legal separation from the Union. But when South Carolina attacked Fort Sumter, on April

12, 1861, that possibility was lost and conflict was made inevitable. Georgia's governor called for volunteers six days later and the Civil War was on. Peter Thompson was fourteen months old.

Slave life during the Civil War varied widely according to location and the financial condition of the slave owner. The war did not come directly—in the form of Union soldiers—to Washington County and Jefferson Counties until well into 1863. But long before that, very early in the war, Georgians and, consequently, their slaves were being adversely impacted. With the trains blocked, most of the foodstuffs that had come into Georgia were stopped almost immediately. And with Union ships blocking all of the Georgia ports, cotton that would have provided income was stacking up on the wharves, unable to get to market.

On the other hand, slavery broke down somewhat during the war. With most of the white men gone off to war and women running the plantations and businesses, slaves used the absence of white males to secure better working and living conditions. And as Union forces made their way into the interior of the state, many slaves ran away to seek their freedom with the advancing Northern troops.

Peter was aware of none of this, of course. No doubt, short rations made for some hungry times. And his parents had some hard choices to make about whether to stay on the plantation or risk running away toward the Union troops—especially after the Emancipation Proclamation officially made them free in the eyes of the

Union forces. But Peter was only two years old when the Emancipation Proclamation was issued, and for him it was all just childhood.

When Union General William T. Sherman made his famous march from Atlanta across Georgia to the sea at Savannah in November and December of 1864, the early trickle of slave runaways became a flood. Thousands of former slaves abandoned their white former owners and followed Sherman's army to actual—as well as official—freedom. Sherman's own path to the sea took him directly through Washington County, Georgia.

On January 16, 1865, General Sherman issued Special Field Order No. 15, a temporary plan that granted each freed family forty acres of tillable land and one of the many mules that had been confiscated in his march across Georgia.

No records exist to tell us if the Thompson family were recipients of land under Special Order No. 15, but for one brief, shining year in one small part of Georgia, the fabled promise of forty acres and a mule for each family of freed slaves was actually true. Unfortunately, about a year later—after Abraham Lincoln's assassination and Vice President Andrew Johnson's becoming President—Johnson terminated Special Order No. 15, and returned all of the land to the original owners.

The Civil War ended when Peter was still only five years old. Freedom of all slaves was now official throughout the land and the United States had installed a military government over Georgia and all of the other Confederate States to protect the rights of the newly freed. Special courts were established to handle disputes or legal issues between the freedmen and the whites and to assist the former slaves in getting established. For the first time, Peter's family lived in a house that they could think of as their own. As with most freedmen, Peter's family went on doing the same kind of farm work they had done as enslaved workers, but now they worked for wages. As soon as he was old enough to handle the work, Peter also went to the fields to help the family.

Both of Peter's parents appear to have died before 1880, and his siblings scattered to their own lives. By age nineteen, Peter was again living in Washington County and was out on his own. He was still working as a farm laborer, but now he was renting his own house with the help of two boarders. Among Peter's neighbors was the Shatteen family, whose daughter Anne soon caught his eye.

Anne M. Shatteen was born about 1866, in Washington County, Georgia, the second child of Mason Shatteen and Sallie Morgan. Anne's parents had been born and raised in slavery, but slavery had finally collapsed under the Civil War and Federal law. Anne, her older sister Linnie (born in 1862), her brother James (born in 1867), and sister Lillian (1868), were all born after slavery ended and grew up on a farm obtained by their father as a free sharecropper. They grew up in the turmoil, hardships, and conflicts of the aftermath of slavery, and never knew the harsh reality of enslavement.

With her parents' consent, Peter Thompson married fifteen-year-old Anne on May 19, 1881, in Washington County, Georgia. The young couple soon set up house in the same neighborhood where they had been living. After two years together, in June of 1883, daughter, Sarah A. Thompson, was born.

Sometime between Sarah's birth and 1900, Anne Shatteen Thompson died. The records that might have told us more about Anne Shatteen's life, or that might have told us exactly how and when she died, simply do not exist for that part of Georgia in that period.

We do know that Anne's widowed husband, Peter, had to continue to work to make a living, and so her daughter, Sarah, went to live with Anne's mother. The 1900 census report shows Peter Thompson back in Jefferson County, Georgia, living with Polly Thompson. His daughter, Sarah, was living with her grandmother, Sallie Shatteen, back in the old neighborhood in Washington County.

After several years as a widower, Peter married again and had other children. He died in Jefferson County, Georgia, between 1930 and 1940. Sarah A. Thompson is the direct ancestor of this family line.

Robert Campbell Forsythe & Nina Washington

Until wealthy foreigners recognized the joy of escaping the snow and ice of winter to sit on the beach of a tropical island, the majority of common people of the Bahama Islands lived in some level of poverty. Since their discovery by the Europeans in the 1600s, many schemes had been brought to the islands in an effort to create an economy that would benefit everyone. Most of them failed and the people stayed poor.

During the early- to mid-1800s, wrecking—salvaging cargos and sometimes passengers from ships that had wrecked on the rocky reefs in the shallow waters around the islands—was a lucrative activity. Then Britain found out that some islanders were going beyond simple salvage and were taking active action to trick ships onto the rocks. The government began regulating the practice and eventually outlawed it all together.

There was a truly wonderful flurry of wealth during the American Civil War while the Confederates used the Bahamian island of New Providence as their base of operations for the blockade-running fleet. But to the islanders' great dissatisfaction, the end of the Civil War also ended the good economic times and triggered what would be the beginning of a fifty-year economic depression.

As fortune would have it, Percy Campbell Forsythe was born on New Providence in St. Agnes Parish on the outskirts of Nassau, the island's largest town. Percy was the first child of Samuel James Forsythe and his young wife, Amelia Deane. He was born on 10 June, 1879, in the fourteenth year of the economic depression engulfing the Bahamas.

Samuel Forsythe was a hotel worker in Nassau, but pay was low and the family was poor. This probably contributed to the hard times that Samuel and Amelia had with their children—in the next few years after Percy's birth, first a daughter and then a son were born, but both died before their first birthday. Finally, in 1885, another son, Samuel James Forsythe, Jr., was born and survived.

Percy grew up in a society where about 85% of the population was black. This was partially the result of Americans with pro-slave English ideals and the large number of slaves that were brought to the Bahamas with the doomed hope of keeping the plantation economy and lifestyle alive.

Others of the majority black population were the descendants of freshly captured Africans who were taken off slaver ships when Britain outlawed the slave trade in 1807. Britain required their navy to stop the slavers and confiscate the human cargoes, which they did with great vigor. The British Navy did not, however, feel obligated to haul the freed Africans all the way back to Africa. Instead, thousands of freed Africans were off-loaded onto the various islands of the British West Indies with a modicum of supplies and with the expectation that they should make do as best they could. In 1834, Britain freed all slaves everywhere in their Empire and the black majority of the West Indies were suddenly all free to seek their fortunes and grow into whatever they could be.

It is no surprise that the white business and land owners comprised the upper social class. But it is surprising that the middle class was made up primarily of light-skinned blacks and the lower class was made up of darker-skinned people. And for a long time, it was not possible for a darker-skinned person to climb out of the lower class and into one of the higher classes—it simply wasn't allowed. It wasn't the same form of harsh discrimination faced by African Americans in America under the Jim Crow laws, but in some ways it was worse. A black American, if he was careful, could improve his own economic and social position within the black community despite white discrimination. In the Bahamas during the Percy's early years, it was almost impossible for a dark-skinned islander to do the same. Under these circumstances, it is easy to see why Percy and his brother, Samuel James, decided to emigrate to America for better opportunities.

According to his own testimony on a petition for U.S. citizenship, Percy Campbell Forsythe stated that he left the Bahamas for America in about 1898. Some records suggest that Percy may have gone first to Nova Scotia, Canada, for a while before moving to Manhattan, New York, but it appears that Samuel James went straight to Manhattan. One thing seems clear: Percy was fascinated by steamships from early on. Shortly after entering America, he found a job with a steamship company, and once he reached a position he liked, he never left.

By 1914, Percy was working in a steamer sailing up and down the east coast of the United States, hauling cargo and passengers between New York and Savannah, Georgia. Percy worked in the kitchens of the ships starting as a pantry man and, over the years,he worked his way up to one of the head cook positions.

At some point—undoubtedly during one of his layovers in Savannah—Percy Forsythe met a young woman named Lula Bachelor, a Savannah native. They apparently got along well, and when his ship turned north toward New York again, she went with him. Percy Campbell Forsythe and Lula Bachelor were married on 27 September, 1915, in Manhattan, New York.

For the next several years, Lula held down the fort at their home in Manhattan while Percy sailed the seas, away from home for days and sometimes weeks at a time. In the early 1920s, he sailed on a ship called the *Cristobal*, making runs from New York to Haiti and back. Later, Percy rejoined the Ocean Steamship Company of Savannah and was soon back on the old route between New York and Savannah, Georgia. Unfortunately, Lula Bachelor Forsythe died unexpectedly a few years later in Manhattan.

Percy Campbell Forsythe continued his work on the New York to Savannah run and some years later met and married Nina Washington, another girl from Savannah. Percy and Nina had two children: Nina Forsythe, born February 24, 1925, and Robert J. Forsythe, born September 15, 1926. Marriage and family were enough to induce Percy to shift his home base from New York City to Savannah, where he could live with the family between sailings. But it was not enough to get him to give up his career on the steamships.

Nina Washington was born October 31, 1908, in Daufuskie, Beaufort County, South Carolina, the daughter of Joseph Washington and Mary Robinson. Nina was less than a year old when the family moved from South Carolina to Savannah, Georgia, where Nina grew up.

Whether he died or left, Nina's father soon disappeared from her life. But her mother, Mary, was an enterprising lady and kept the family housed and fed by running a boarding house and lunch room—she prepared more food for lunch than was needed for her boarders and sold it to the local public. Her older brother Albert, who continued to live at home until his marriage, was a blacksmith who also helped meet expenses for the family.

Nina worked as a cook's helper after she went out on her on, but she also followed in her mother's footsteps and took in boarders. That is probably how she met Percy Campbell Forsythe. With time off between sailings—while the ship was being refueled and new cargo was being loaded—he would have needed a place to stay. The combination of interest and proximity came together, and marriage occurred.

Having regularly spent time in Savannah during his employment with a company named Ocean Shipping of Savannah, Percy quickly settled into his new life there. In July of 1941, possibly with an eye toward retirement and living out his life in his adopted country, Percy filed a petition with the United States District Court at Savannah to become an American citizen.

A little over four months later, the Japanese bombed Pearl Harbor and everybody's world shifted a bit. Shortly after the United States declared war on Japan, and recognizing an immediate need for the ability to move men and materials sooner than a new Naval fleet could be created, the United States essentially drafted all major U.S. shipping into the Merchant Marine. Percy's job did not really change, except that now passenger service was sharply curtailed and priority was giving to hauling strategic materials that would best support America's war effort.

It was a necessary step, but one that turned out to be an unfortunate one for Percy Campbell Forsythe. On 19 January, 1942, his ship, the *City of Atlanta* was in the middle of a run from New York to Savannah. The ship was unarmed and had no military escorts. It was just off the coast of North Carolina, running closer to the coast than usual in an effort to reduce the likelihood of attack by German submarines. The tactic did not succeed.

Just after 9:00 p.m., the *City of Atlanta* was hit by one torpedo from the German U-Boat U-123. The torpedo was a surface runner and struck the *City of Atlanta* at the waterline. The ship quickly took on water and began to list onto its side, making it very difficult for the crew of eight officers and 38 crewmen to abandon ship. The vessel rolled completely over and went down in about ten minutes, long before any of the four lifeboats could be launched. Percy Campbell Forsythe and all but three of his shipmates were killed. When help finally arrived about six hours later, only one officer and two men were found clinging to wreckage. The officer later died of his injuries.

Needless to say, Percy's death impacted the family greatly. Ten months after his death, Percy's son, Robert, ran off and lied about his age to join the U.S. Navy. And sadly, Nina Washington Forsythe survived her husband, Percy, by only two and a half years. She died in a Savannah, Georgia, hospital on August 5, 1944. The line continues through Robert J. Forsythe, the son of Percy and Nina Forsythe.

Frederick Curry & Elizabeth Brown

Frederick Curry was born on George Washington's birthday—February 22—in 1907. It was an unusually cold winter day in Savannah, Chatham County, Georgia, where winter days were usually fairly mild.

The ninth child of Duncan Curry and Elizabeth Alston, Frederick was born into an already large and active family, with three older brothers and five older sisters: William was born first, followed by Elizabeth, Ira, Hilda (who died in infancy), Rosa Leola, Solomon, and Edmonia. And Frederick was not the last child—brothers Frampton and Charles came along after Frederick, rounding out the siblings to an even ten.

Frederick's father, Duncan, supported this large brood by doing heavy labor, first for the railroads and later on the docks at Savannah's harbor. With a little help from the older children, the family just got by.

But financial hardships were the least of the troubles for most black Georgians in those days. Those years of the early 1900s were tough, tense times for the black people of Georgia. It was Frederick's bad luck to have been born into some of the harshest of all the Jim Crow segregation years.

In September of 1906, just months before Frederick was born, three of Atlanta's evening newspapers ran featured stories of alleged rapes by black men.

Whites in Atlanta went on a "revenge" spree. When the dust settled after several days of violence and bloodshed—later known as the Atlanta Race Riot—twenty-five blacks and one white were confirmed dead. Several dozens more had been injured, and sources suggested that the casualty count was actually much higher.

Six years later, in 1912, in Forsyth County, a black teenager confessed to the rape and murder of a white girl. After a week of inflammatory reporting by three county newspapers, local whites rioted against local blacks. Three black men were hanged the first night, which was followed by a campaign of terror by night riders. Black-owned houses were dynamited and black churches were burned. More than ninety percent of the black population were told to "leave or die." In the end, it was a successful use of terror to drive more than one-thousand blacks completely out of their homes and out of the county. To this day, Forsyth County is still one of the whitest counties in Georgia.

The City of Savannah was not a place where such large-scale and violent racial drama took place during those years—the first reported Savannah race riot did not happen until 1963 during the protests to end segregation. Instead, during the first half of the twentieth century, Savannah was a place where both races lived through a kind of stylized behavioral dance that was beginning to play out all over the South. The whites taught their children how to carry themselves and how to act toward blacks, to keep "the coloreds in their place" while trying to stop short of inciting a violent reaction. Black people simultaneously taught their children how to avoid eye contact, and to say "yes sir" and "no ma'am" to all whites, even those younger than themselves. They taught the children to play the part that the whites wanted to see while living their own lives the best they could.

This uncomfortable existence went on in the midst of Jim Crow segregation, and the lack of major racial conflagrations allowed Savannah to present itself to the world as a more cosmopolitan city—one that did not really have a "colored problem." But every black person living there knew how strongly racism still thrived and how it was still taking large, if less obvious, bites out of black lives. And the threat of violence, while not always obvious, was constantly there.

In June of 1914, the lives of the Curry family suddenly and unexpectedly got even harder, both emotionally and financially. Just four months after Frederick's seventh birthday, his father, Duncan Curry, died. The older children stepped up and initially took on most of the burden of earning the family living. Two of the girls worked in a local match factory and the older boys found jobs as laborers. When Frederick got old enough, he did his part by going to work as a laborer in a fertilizer plant.

It was while working in this job that Frederick met and took a liking to the girl next door. Frederick and seventeen year-old Elizabeth Brown hit it off and

Frederick was soon courting her in earnest. Elizabeth accepted his interest and, later, his proposal. Frederick and Elizabeth were married in September of 1928.

Elizabeth Brown was born in June of 1911 in Allendale, Barnwell County, South Carolina. She was the daughter of Joseph Brown and Nancy Frazier, and the first of what would eventually become that couple's ten children. Like Elizabeth, her parents had grown up in Allendale and had made a life for their new family there.

But for much of his life, Joseph Brown earned his living as a farm laborer, and times were getting difficult for farmers in Georgia. Much of South Georgia still had cotton as their major cash crop, but then in 1915, the boll weevil hit the area, devastating crops. From there, things just got worse for the farmer—competition from new made-made fabrics, overproduction by farmers trying to make up earlier losses, and the continuing effects of the boll weevil hit the price of cotton hard. By the mid-1920s, workers like Joseph Brown were finding it hard to earn a steady living. Eventually, Joseph Brown gave up on his home town and moved his family to Savannah, seeking better economic opportunities.

Unfortunately, his timing was terrible. A little over a year after Frederick and Elizabeth Brown's marriage, the beginning of the Great Depression hit the entire country, and like millions of other Americans—both black and white—Joseph Brown found himself out of work again. By 1930, both Joseph and Nancy Brown were out of work and living next door to their new son-in-law and seven of their minor children. Frederick still had that one hugely valuable thing that year—a job.

Frederick Curry proved himself a hardworking and responsible man when he took on the task of supporting his new wife's minor siblings. He supported this crowd, along with his own increasing family, by working as a laborer in Savannah's Virginia-Carolina Chemical Company, a fertilizer plant.

The economy remained poor throughout the 1930s and real recovery did not start until the beginning of World War II. There were small pockets of improvement, though, and these small changes allowed Elizabeth Brown Curry's siblings to begin their move out of the Curry household. Some went to new marriages, some moved out on their own, and some went in together and lived with one another until the economy recovered.

By 1940, Frederick and Elizabeth were back to having only their own family living in the household. This was a good thing for the Currys because while the aunts and uncles were growing up and moving out, the Curry family was just plain growing on its own. Frederick and Elizabeth's first child, daughter Lucretia Jo Curry, was born on March 5, 1929, but she did not stay an only child for very long. Sister Nancy was born in 1931, and brother Frederick Curry, Jr., followed on August 18, 1936.

Frederick's job with the Virginia-Carolina Chemical Company had protected his family against the very worst of the Depression—though wages and perks dropped with the economy. With the Japanese attack on Pearl Harbor and America's entry into World War II, the Virginia-Carolina Chemical Company began to expand into new fields. It went through a few corporate name changes, but operations kept growing and expanding into many divisions in several states. For Frederick, this more or less assured him of indefinite full-time employment. Toward the end of the 1930s he had been moved into a job as a tractor operator for the company's plant in Savannah. It turned out to be a position that he was to keep for the rest of his working days.

Like all families, the Currys had their successes and their failures. After WWII, they just settled down and got on with life. They watched their children grow up and go out to seek their new lives as adults.

Neither Frederick nor Elizabeth Curry lived long lives. But in their lifetimes they had seen some subtle changes in the humiliating behavioral dance that black people were forced to perform during their long segregation. And near the end of their lives, they got to see the beginning of the end for segregation—the 1963 street protests in Savannah where black men did not step off the sidewalk to let white people pass; where black men came before the whites, not with their hats in hand or with downward cast eyes, but with their heads up. They saw black people come into the streets, not asking for favors, but demanding their rightful place in the American story. Perhaps it was enough to allow them to them see the beginning of a new future.

Frederick Curry died in Savannah on November 13, 1964, at the age of 57 years. He was buried in Laurel Grove Cemetery in Savannah, Georgia. Elizabeth Brown Curry outlived her husband by about 11 months, and died on October 16, 1965, in Savannah, Chatham County, Georgia. She was also buried in Laurel Grove Cemetery in Savannah. Frederick Curry and Elizabeth Brown's first child, Lucretia Jo Curry, is the direct line ancestor of this family line.

CITATIONS

The following is a complete source citations of all genealogies from the TFH compilation, broken down into the Thompson (Sources A) and the Curry (Sources B).

.

SOURCES A:

1 Gerald G Thompson, Middletown, PA, June, 2010.1 Shirley Mary Duncan, #1487170-1935, 11-29-1935, Snyder Co, PA, Department of Vital Records, New Castle, PA.

2 Gerald Gilbert Thompson birth record, #1170270-1935, 09-23-1935, Dauphin Co, PA, Department of Vital Records, New Castle, PA.

3 Harper Bruce Thompson birth record, #344701, #122649-07, September 1907, Schuylkill Co, PA, Department of Vital Records, New Castle, PA.

4 Harper B Thompson death certificate, #2501265, Department of Vital Records, New Castle, PA.

5 Harper B Thompson, Obituary, Harrisburg Patriot Newspaper, July 1981.

6 Thompson-Batdorf marriage record, Register of Wills, Clerk of Orphans Court, Dauphin Co, PA, 1935.

7 Samuel Peters, Descendants of John Peters, Evelyn S. Hartman.

8 Myrtle A. Batdorf birth certificate, January 1918, Department of Vital records, New Castle, PA.

9 Myrtle Thompson, Obituary, Harrisburg Patriot newspaper, 1983.

10 Myrtle A Thompson death certificate, #3455802, Department of Vital records, New Castle, PA.

11 Duncan family information, Jack Lehman, North Charleston, SC.

12 William Duncan, April 1978, PA, Social Security Death Index, www.familysearch.org.

13 Irvin Francis Duncan, Birth record, Northumberland Co County Courthouse, Register of Wills, Sunbury, PA.

14 Irvin Duncan, April 1978, PA, Social Security Death Index, www.familysearch.org.

15 Irvin Francis Duncan death certificate, #0030831, Northumberland Co, PA, Department of Vital Records, New Castle, PA.

16 Mary Lucetta Anderson, Memoranda, Bob Anderson, PA, rmorris@ptd.net.

17 Mamie Duncan, April 1989, PA, Social Security Death Index, www.familysearch.org.

18 Mamie Lucetta Duncan death certificate, #0078833, #069201, April 1989, Department of Vital Record, New Castle, PA.

19 Mamie Luzetta Anderson, #061660-1908, 04-13-1908, Northumberland Co, PA, Department of Vital Records, New Castle, PA.

20 Mamie L Duncan, Probate file, 47-89-85, microfiche, Montour County Courthouse, Office of the Reg and Recorder, Danville, PA, Norman Nicol, ndnicol@epix.net, Mar 2008.

21 Abel Thompson death certificate, #0506211, #133775-93, January 1918, Department of Vital Records, New castle, PC.

22 Thompson-Hensel Marriage, Office of the Register of Wills, Schuylkill County, PA, June 1904.

23 Abel Robert Thompson, WW I Draft Reg Cards, 1917-1918 Record, www.ancestry.com.

24 Abel R Thompson, Probate file, 1918, unnumbered original papers, 34pp, Schuylkill Co Courthouse, Schuylkill, PA, Norman Nicol, Apr 2008.

25 Gussie May Thompson death certificate, #0506187, #31982, March 1973, Department of Vital Records, New Castle, PA.

26 Gussie May Hensel, Funeral obituary, March 1973.

27 Gussie Mae Thompson, Obituary, Pottsville Repulbican, Pottsville, PA, March 28, 1973.

28 Gussie M. Thompson, Greenwood Cemetery, Tower City, Schuylkill Co, PA, John Barket, Tower City, PA, B-3-1.

29 Gussie M. Thompson, Reg of Will book, Book 145, pp578-82, May 27, 1950, probated Sept 11, 1973, Schuylkill Co Courthouse, Schuylkill, PA, Norman Nicol, Apr 2008.

30 Michael Goodman, Descendants of Michael Goodman, Evelyn S Hartman, deanh@voicenet.com.

31 Abel F Thompson, Bob Averell Family Tree, Entries: 7956, Updated: 2004-08-01 00:29:03 UTC (Sun), Contact: Bob Averell.

32 Lydia Mae Thompson, Obituary, Pottsville Repulbican, Pottsville, PA, Jan 18, 1983.

33 James Edward Batdorf death certificate, #0506183, #66234-39, August 1954, Department of Vital Records, New Castle, PA.

4 James Edward Batdorf, Church record, Rev. O.S. Moyer, Angie Eddy, Maple Grove Cemetery, Eluzabethville, PA, p 29.

35 James Edward Batdorf, United States WW II Draft Reg. Cards, 1942 Record, 2243624, www.ancestry.com.

36 James Edward Batdorf, Social Security numident record, application for SS-5, SSA, Nov 2006, Baltimore, MD.

37 Batdorf-Wert marriage record, Church record, Rev. O.S. Moyer, Angie Eddy, Maple Grove Cemetery, Elizabethville, PA, p 16.

38 Beulah I Batdorf death certificate, #0506188, #057537, June 1983, Department of Vital records, New Castle, PA.

39 Beulah Batdorf, June 1983, PA, Social Security Death Index, www.familysearch.org.

40 Beulah I Batdorf, Obituary, Harrisburg Patriot News, 1983.

41 John Peters, Peters family information, Evelyn S Hartman, deanh@voicenet.com.

42 Peter Batdorf, Descendants of Peter Batdorf, Evelyn S Hartman, deanh@voicenet.com.

43 Duncan-Layman mariage record, #8855, Northumberland Co, PA, 1899, Northumberland Co County Register of Wills.

44 Wm Duncan death certificate, #0030852, #90924, Northumberland Co, PA, Department of Vital records, New Castle, PA.

45 Duncan family information, Stephanie Gormley.

46 Duncan-Layman marriage record, April 20, 1899, Edward C. Eisley.

47 Duncan-Layman marriage record, #8855, Northumberland Co, PA, 1899, Northumberland Co County Register of Wills, Sunbury, PA.

48 Duncan-Layman marriage record, #8855, Northumberland Co, PA, 1899, Northumberland Co County Register of Wills.

49 Lottie V. Willard, death certificate, File #29987, Reg #19, #3505042, February 1936, Department of Vital Records, New Castle, PA.

50 William Duncan, Pomfret Manor Cemetery, Sunbury, Northumberland Co, PA, NCHS, The Hunter House, Sunbury, PA.

51 Duncan household, 1900 United States Census, microfilm image, PA State Library. Died Sunbury, PA, Duncan family information, Stephanie Gormley.

52 Charlotte Layman, Duncan family information, Stephanie Gormley.

53 Anderson-Keefer marriage record, Northumberland Co, PA, Northumberland Co Register of Wills, #11421.

54 William Anderson, May 1969, PA, Social Security Death Index, www.familysearch.org.

55 William Morris Anderson death certificate, #0740733, #050910-69, May 1969, Department of Vital Records, New Castle, PA.

56 William M. Anderson, Cemetery records, Orchard Hills Cemetery and Memorial Park, Shamokin Dam, PA, Janet, Section 3, Lot 188.

57 Anderson-Keefer marriage record, July 15, 1902, Northumberland Co, PA, Northumberland Co Register of Wills, #11421.

58 Bible p, Marriage records, source unknown.

59 Memoranda, Bob Anderson, PA, rmorris@ptd.net.

60 Emma L. Keefer, Bible p, Birth records, source unknown.

61 Emma Louisa Anderson death certificate, #0740677, #53801-503, April 1963, Department of Vital Records, New Castle, PA.

62 Emma Louisa Keefer, Northumberland Co, PA, 1861-92, Zion Evangelical Lutheran Church, search.ancesry.com.

63 Emma Louisa Anderson death certificate, #0740677, #53801-503, April 1963, Department of Vital Records, New Castle, PA.

64 Emma L. Anderson, Cemetery records, Orchard Hills Cemetery and Memorial Park, Shamokin Dam, PA, Janet, Section 3, Lot 188.

65 William Morris Anderson, #0740733, #050910-69, May 1969, Department of Vital Records, New Castle, PA.

66 William Maurice Anderson, U.S. World War 1 Draft Registration Cards, No 1674, 3-27-0, Snyder, PA, 1917, www.ancestry.com.

67 Emma L. Anderson, Emma Louise Anderson, obituary, Sunbury newspaper.

68 Robert B Thompson death certificate, #0042512, #102079, Reg # 102, October 1907, Department of Vital records, New Castle, PA.

69 Robert B Thompson, Greenwood Cemetery, Tower City, Schuylkill Co, PA, John Barket, Tower City, PA, B-1-1.

70 Thompson family information, John L linden, jllinden@comcast.net.

71 Alexander Thompson, Schuylkill County, PA, p 1054.

72 Lydia B. Thompson, Greenwood Cemetery, Tower City, Schuylkill Co, PA, John Barket, Tower City, PA, B-1-1.

73 Bob Averell Family Tree, Bob Averell, raverell@carolina.rr.com, awt.ancestry.com.

74 Howard A.C. Hensel, #0036895, #63360, Reg # 66, June 1927, Department of Vital records, New Castle, PA.

75 Hensel family information, Victor Hensel, NJ.

76 Howard Andrew Carson Hensel, Howard Andrew Carson Hensel probate file, 1927, unnumbered orginal papers, 21pp, probated June 29, 1927, Schuylkill Co Courthouse, Schuylkill, PA, Norman Nicol, Apr 2008.

77 Clara M Hensel death certificate, #0042528, #37124, Reg # 29, March 1926, Department of Vital records, New Castle, PA.

78 Casper Hansel, Descendants of Casper (LaHentzelle) Hensel, Evelyn S Hartman, deanh@voicenet.com.

79 Batdorf Family information, Virginia Faust.

80 Thomas Batdorf, #0102590, #81400-17, 1916, Department of Vital records, New Castle, PA.

81 Mary L Batdorf, #0042526, #7?-23, 1924, Department of Vital records, New Castle, PA.

82 John Wert, #0042527, #95868-1303, 1924, Department of Vital records, New Castle, PA.

83 Adeline Row, St. John Evangelical Lutheran Church, Berrysburg, PA, Sara S. Neagley, Elizabethville, PA. 84 Mrs. Adeline Wert death certificate, #26162, #3457526, March 1921, Department of Vital Records, New Castle, PA.

85 Descendants of Frederick Adam Faber, Evelyn S Hartman, deanh@voicenet.com.

86 Johann Heinrich Friedrich Dankert, Ancestry.com. Germany, Select Births and Baptisms, 1558-1898 [database on-line]. Deutschland, Geburten und Taufen 1558-1898 Germany, Select Births and Baptisms, 1558-1898, Provo, UT, USA: Ancestry.com Operations, Inc., 2014. Original data: Germany, Births and Baptisms, 1558-1898. Salt Lake City, Utah: FamilySearch, 2013.

87 Catherine Duncan, Death certificate, Northumberland Co County Register of Wills, Sunbury, PA.

88 Duncan family information, Stephanie Gormley, PA, 1989.

89 Melinda Duncan, Cemetery record, Apr 1933, A genealogists Guide to Burials in Northumberland Co, PA, Vol I, Meiser & Meiser, 1989.

90 Sallie Duncan, Cemetery record, Apr 1933, A genealogists Guide to Burials in Northumberland Co, PA, Vol I, Meiser & Meiser, 1989.

91 Sarah Duncan, Baptisms of Infants, Zion Evan Luth Register, 1851-1892, Sunbury, PA, p41.

92 Hannah Artilla Duncan, Baptisms of Infants, Zion Evan Luth Register, 1851-1892, Sunbury, PA, p94.

93 Charley Duncan, Baptisms of Infants, Zion Evan Luth Register, 1851-1892, Sunbury, PA, p101.

94 Layman/Lehman family information, Files, NCHS, The Hunter House, Sunbury, PA.

95 Joseph Pierce Layman, death record, Illinois Statewide Death Index, 1916-1950, www.cyberdriveillinois.com/GenealogyMWeb/ODPHdeathsearch.

96 Joseph Pierce Layman, State of IL, Dept of Public Health, DVS, Reg #4976, Primary Dt #3104, Cook, IL, Feb 1924.

97 Lehman-Oberlander marriage, source unknown.

98 Rebecca Lehman (Layman) death certificate, #105066, Reg # 456, #3457529, November 1921, Department of Vital Records, New   Castle,   PA.

99 Lucetta Anderson death certificate, #0740660, #117712-223, November 1916, Department of Vital records, New Castle, PA.

100 Anderson family information, Stephanie Gormley, PA.

101 Bible p, Birth records, source unknown.

102 James P Keefer death record abstract, August 4, 1892, Edward C. Eisley.

103 Thompson family information, Jim Thompson, jbthompson@compuserve.com, pp 4-11.

104 Thompson family information, Films from 1993, Jane L Fouraker, Lancaster Co, PA.

105 Thompson family information, Jim Thompson, jbthompson@compuserve.com, pp 4-11 & Thompson family information, Irene C. Stearns, DeKalb, IL.

106 Isabel Penman, Vital records Index, British Isles, Intellectual Reserve Inc, 8/5/2010.

107 Thompson family information, Irene C. Stearns, DeKalb, IL.

108 Alexander Thompson, Schuylkill County, PA, p 668-669.

109 Alexander Thompson, Miners Journal, December 5, 1873.

110 Mrs. Thompson, Burial record, Miners Journal deaths, 1851.

111 Michael Goodman, Tower City, Porter Centennial, 1868-1968, p 188.

112 Michael Goodman, Obituatary, FROM 'THE WEST SCHUYLKILL HERALD', 03 JANUARY 1901, Jeffrey A. Brown, ntrprz@dmv.com.

113 Michael Gurtmann, "Pennsylvania, Births and Christenings, 1709-1950," index, FamilySearch (https://familysearch.org/pal:/MM9.1.1/V2NX-KXS : accessed 19 Nov 2014), Michael Gutmann, 12 May 1811; Christening, citing SAINT JOHNS LUTHERAN CHURCH NEAR BERRYSBURG,MIFFLIN TWP,DAUPHIN,PENNSYLVANIA; FHL microfilm 845111.

114 Michael Goodman death certificate, #1252, May 1901, Dauphin County Register of Wills, Harrisburg, PA.

115 Hensel-Workman marriage record, 1853, Register of Wills, Dauphin Co, PA.

116 Hensel family information, Dauphin Co Marriages, 1852-1855, CAGS.

117 Hensel family information, History of Michael Hensel (Hentzel) Sr. & His Related Families, R. Longtin-Thompson.

118 Andrew Gise Hensel death certificate, #0036891, #115081, Reg # 84, December 1908, Department of Vital records, New Castle, PA.

119 Andrew Gise Hensel, #0036891, #115081, Reg # 84, December 1908, Department of Vital records, New Castle, PA.

120 Daniel Updegrove death certificate, #1071, March 1899, Dauphin County Register of Wills, Harrisburg, PA.

121 Updegrove Family information, Updegrove Genealogy, PA State library.

122 Daniel Updegrove, Vital records, Dauphin County, p 26.

123 Mrs. Sarah Updegrove death certificate, #0042525, #81494, File 42, Reg 2193, July 1923, Department of Vital Records, New Castle, PA.

124 Welkers in the USA & Nulls from PA, Greg Welker, gwelker@chesapeake.net, awt.ancestry.com.

125 Baddorf Family, Gratz History, p 193.

126 Peter Batdorf, St. Peters (Hoffmans) Union Church, Burials.

127 Peter Botdorf, St. Peter's (Hoffman's) Union Church, Lykens, Dauphin Co, PA, Gert Mysliwski, gert@foothill.net.

128 Peter Batdorf, Hoffmans Reformed Church, Lykens Valley, Dauphin Co, PA, Historical & Genealogical, pp 227-8.

129 Peter Batdorf, Probate files, 1881, Affidavit Rep #5, Dauphin County Courthouse, Reg of Wills, Deborah Hershey, Elizabethtown, PA, Mar 2008.

130 Elizabeth Batdorf, Hoffmans Reformed Church, Lykens Valley, Dauphin Co, PA, Historical & Genealogical, pp 227-8.

131 Mary Peters death certificate, bk C, #945, 1897, Dauphin County Register of Wills, Harrisburg, PA.

132 Mary Peters death certificate, Dauphin County Register of Wills, bk C, #945, 1897, Harrisburg, PA, 140, bk C, #945, 1897, Perry County Historians.

133 Mary Peters death certificate, Dauphin County Register of Wills, bk C, #945, 1897, Harrisburg, PA.

134 Wert Family, Jonathan Wert.

135 David Wert death certificate, Dauphin County Register of Wills, bk E, #852, December 20, 1900, , Harrisburg, PA.

136 Shoop family information, Are you my cousin, Howard Ward, haroldw1@juno.com, awt.ancestry.com.

137 Monn & Related Families, Danni Monn Hopkins, clueless@clnk.com, awt.ancestry.com.

138 David Wert (West) death record, Extract from County Death records, 1893-1906.

139 Wert household, 1870 United States Census, Dauphin Co, PA, PA State library microfilm.

140 Wertz family information, Bob Messerschmidt, Laurel, MD, SusanM4383@aol.com.

141 Wertz family information, Cindi Grimm, Grimm@ruralife.net.

142 Daniel Row, Baptismal record, St. John Evangelical Lutheran Church, Dauphin Co, PA, p 64.

143 Rowe family information, Howard E Row, Dover, DE.

144 Daniel Rowe, St. John Evangelical Lutheran Church, Berrysburg, PA, Sara S. Neagley, Elizabethville, PA, 424 6M 24D.

145 Susanna Rowe, St. John Evangelical Lutheran Church, Berrysburg, PA, Sara S. Neagley, Elizabethville, PA.

146 Joh Heinr Dankert, Mecklenburg-Schwerin Volkszählung, 1819 Mecklenburg-Schwerin, Germany, Ancestry.com. Mecklenburg-Schwerin, Germany, Census, 1819 [database on-line]. Provo, UT, USA: Ancestry.com Operations Inc, 2007. Original data: Mecklenburg-Schwerin (Großherzogtum), Volkszählungsamt. Volkszählung 1819. Landeshauptarchiv Schwerin. 2.21-4/4 Bevölkerungs-, Geburts-,Konfirmations-, Heirats- und Sterbelisten.

147 Gerhard Wilhelm Heinrich Dankert, Deutschland, Geburten und Taufen 1558-1898 Germany, Select Births and Baptisms, 1558-1898 Ancestry.com. Germany, Select Births and Baptisms, 1558-1898 [database on-line]. Provo, UT, USA: Ancestry.com Operations, Inc., 2014. Original data: Germany, Births and Baptisms, 1558-1898. Salt Lake City, Utah: FamilySearch, 2013.

148 Sophia Magaretha Qualmann, Mecklenburg-Schwerin Volkszählung, 1819 Mecklenburg-Schwerin, Germany, Census, 1819 Ancestry.com. Mecklenburg-Schwerin, Germany, Census, 1819 [database on-line]. Provo, UT, USA: Ancestry.com Operations Inc, 2007.

149 Carolina Maria Henriette Kelling, Deutschland, Geburten und Taufen 1558-1898 Germany, Select Births and Baptisms, 1558-1898, Ancestry.com. Germany, Select Births and Baptisms, 1558-1898 [database on-line]. Provo, UT, USA: Ancestry.com Operations, Inc., 2014. Original data: Germany, Births and Baptisms, 1558-1898. Salt Lake City, Utah: FamilySearch, 2013.

150 Caroline Maria Henriette Kelling, Deutschland, Tote und Beerdigungen 1582-1958 Germany, Select Deaths and Burials, 1582-1958 Ancestry.com. Germany, Select Deaths and Burials, 1582-1958 [database on-line]. Provo, UT, USA: Ancestry.com Operations, Inc., 2014. Original data: Germany, Deaths and Burials, 1582-1958. Salt Lake City, Utah: FamilySearch, 2013.

151 David McCord, Family tree. https://familysearch.org/tree/#view=tree&person=935Q-7XG&section=pedigree, familysearch.org.

152 David McCloud, Probate files, 1864, Northumberland County Courthouse, Reg of Wills, Sunbury, Bk 5, p261, PA, Robyn Jackson, genealogylover@msn.com, 2008.

153 Jeremiah McCloud, Pennsylvania, Death Certificates, 1906-1924 forJeremiah McCloud, ancestry.com.

154 McCloud-Frye, Marriage, Northumberland County, SS, #2856, Register & Recorder, Sunbury, PA, Oct 1890, Market St, Sunbury, PA.

155 Michael Layman, Bethel ME Cemetery, p 151, Jerome K. Hively, Brogue, PA.

156 Elmira Layman, Bethel ME Cemetery, p 151, Jerome K. Hively, Brogue, PA.

157 Duncan family information, 1870 United States Census, York Co, PA, Roll M593-1468, p 545, Image 700, ancestry.com & Microfilm, PA State Library, Hbg, PA.

158 Overlander-Kipe marriage record, #662-59, Calender of Vital Records of the Counties of York & Adams.

159 Sarah Oberlander, Probate files, 1874, Rep 42, York County Archives, York, PA, Deborah Hershey, Elizabethtown, PA, Dec 2008.

160 Casper Arnold, Crossley/Gunsallus/Kimmel Family, Worldconnect Project, worldconnect.rootsweb.com.

161 Anderson family information, Jim Anderson, Ontario, CAN.

162 Elijah Anderson, January 1820, Record of Grubb's (Botschaft) Lutheran Church, 1792-1875.

163 Elijah Anderson, Tombstone Incriptions of Snyder County, PA, M.B. Lontz, 1981.

164 Arnold family information, Snyder County pioneers, Snyder County.

165 Family Ties, Laurie Lendosky, llendosky@cyberia.com, awt.ancestry.com/cgi-bin/igm-cgi.

166 Cath. Anderson, 1893, Tombstone Inscriptions of Snyder County, PA, M.B. Lontz, 1981, Union County Historical Society.

167 Catherine Anderson, Letters of Adminstration, 1893, Snyder County Courthouse, Register of Wills.

168 Anderson family information, Stephanie Gormley, PA & Descendants of Philip Jacob Bordner, John Getz, jgetz@iu.net.

169 Croce/Walker Family Tree, Sue Walker, smawalker@comcast.net, awt.ancestry.com.

170 Abraham Gaugler death certificate, August 1900, Snyder County Register of Wills, Middleburg, PA.

171 Abraham Gaugler, Obituary, Middleburg Post, Thu Aug 30, 1900, c/o Pat Smith, pms9848@hotmail.com.

172 Some of my ancestors, David A. Miller, david.miller@nwa.com, awt.ancestry.com.

173 Kelly family information, Sue Dufour, sdufour@skyenet.net.

174 Kesiah Gaugler, Mount Zion United Brethren Church Cemetery, Snyder Co, PA, Shaffer & Arnold, 1904, www.rootsweb.com.

175 Mrs Annie Duttry, Pennsylvania, Death Certificates, Ancestry.com. Pennsylvania, Death Certificates, 1906-1963 [database on-line]. Provo, UT, USA: Ancestry.com Operations, Inc., 2014.

176 Gougler/Thursby family information, Jean Doherty, jmd17601@yahoo.com.

177 Kieffer family information, www.geocities.com/jimmyk418/surname.htm.

178 Family of Eldon G. Keefer, Eldon G. Keefer, PeterKeefer@aol.com, awt.keefer.com.

179 Kieffer family information, Family Group record, Jere S. Keefer, Mercersburg, PA.

180 M.A. Keefer death certificate, February 1904, Northumberland Co County Register of Wills, Sunbury, PA.

181 Michael A. Keefer, Spruce St. Cemetery, Sunbury, Northumberland Co County Historical Society.

182 Keefer, Kiefer file, Northumberland Co County Historical Society, Sunbury, PA, Floyd, p 346.

183 Margaret M Keefer death certificate, April 1899, Northumberland Co County Register of Wills, Sunbury, PA.

184 Margaret M. Keefer, Spruce St. Cemetery, Sunbury, Northumberland Co County Historical Society.

185 Margaret M Keefer death record abstract, April 1899, Edward C. Eisley.

186 Margaret M Keefer death record, May 6, 1899, Northumberland Co County Register of Wills, PA, Sunbury, PA.

187 Margaret M Keefer, Obituary, Sunbury newspaper, Robert C. Eisley.

188 Michael A. Keefer, Spruce St. Cemetery, Sunbury, Northumberland Co County Historical Society.

189 Michael A. Keefer, Keefer, Kiefer files, Northumberland Co County Historical Society, Sunbury, PA.

190 Keefer family information, Family of Eldon G. Keefer, Eldon G. Keefer, PeterKeefer@aol.com, awt.keefer.com.

191 The Livezey Family, Sixth Generation, The Livezey Association, p 152.

192 Anna M Livezly, Death record, 388, Aug 1910, Warren, Massachusetts, Connie Taylor <connieataylor@icloud.com>.

193 Livezty household, 1900 Census, "Livetzly" household, 1900 United States Federal Census, SD 6, ED 147, Sheet 12, Cumberland, NJ, www.ancestry.com & Microfilm, PA State Library, Hbg, PA.

194 Livezty household, 1900 United States Federal Census, SD 6, ED 147, Sheet 12, Cumberland, NJ, www.ancestry.com & Microfilm, PA State Library, Hbg, PA.

195 Robert Thompson, Ancestry Publci trees, O'Brien Family Tree, Owner: christine hillstead, ancestry.com.

196 Thompson family information, Jane Fouraker, mjfour@mindpsring.com.

197 Robert Thompson, Thompson History, Jim Thompson, jbthompson@compuserve.com, pp 4-11, Thompson family information, John B. Linden, Lynden@comcast.net.

198 Penman family information, Jim Thompson, jbthompson@compuserve.com.

199 David Penman, FHL, Pedigree chart, www.ancestry.com.

200 David Penman, Penman family information, John Penman, PenmanJC@aol.com.

201 John Penman, Vital records Index, British Isles, Intellectual Reserve Inc, 8/5/2010.

202 Goodman family data, DESCENDANTS OF GEORGE GOODMAN OF BETHEL TOWNSHIP, BERKS CO, Lawrence Goodman, lawrenceeg@comcast.net, http://www.goodmangenealogy.com/1104.htm.

203 Michael Gudman, Bethel. January 25, 1810. http://berks.pa-roots.com/.

204 Peter Brown, Tyson Family_2012-03-18, Owner: Gary Tyson, ancestry.com.

205 Brown family information, Peter Brown descedants, Deb Kandybowksi, debkandy@epix.net.

206 Andreas Hansel, Baptism, York Co, PA library, cards on file.

207 Andrew Hensel, Christ Church, Littlestown, PA, Adams Co County 18th records lookup, Virginia, vperry1@shawneelink.net.

208 Andrew Hensel, Death of an Old Soldier, Obituary, New Bloomfield newspaper, July 1875.

209 Andrew Hensel, Source 146, index card, Perry County Historians.

210 Mrs. Hensel, Source 140 & 146, index cards, Perry County Historians.

211 Mrs. Mary Hensel, New Bloomfield Times, January 20, 1877.

212 Mary Hensel, U.S., Find A Grave Index, 1600s, Ancestry.com. U.S., Find A Grave Index, 1600s-Current [database on-line]. Provo, UT, USA: Ancestry.com Operations, Inc., 2012. Original data: Find A Grave. Find A Grave. http://www.findagrave.com/cgi-bin/fg.cgi.

213 Workman family information, Evelyn Hartman, Evelyn S Hartman, deanh@voicenet.com.

214 Joseph Workman, Wiconisco Calvary Cemetery, Rhonda, yeahbaby@penn.com, Row 4.

215 Joseph Workman, U.S., Find A Grave Index, 1600s, Ancestry.com. U.S., Find A Grave Index, 1600s-Current [database on-line]. Provo, UT, USA: Ancestry.com Operations, Inc., 2012. Original data: Find A Grave. Find A Grave. http://www.findagrave.com/cgi-bin/fg.cgi.

216 ibid.

217 The Romberger Line, Ancestors of Richard Alan Lebo.

218 Romberger Family, St. John's Lutheran Church, p 10, John Romberger.

219 Johann Uptegrav, 1805, Jacobs Church, Pine Grove, Swedberg, SCUR III, p 240.

220 Updegrove Family information, Rosie Byard, rbyard@bigfoot.com.

221 John Upderove, Smith Family Tree, Owner: hannibal8901, ancestry.com.

222 Rutzel Family Genealogy, David Rutzel, leztur@hotmail.com, awt.ancestry.com.

223 Elizabeth Reiss, Provizzi Family Tree, Owner: sprovizzi, ancestry.com.

224 Kulp family information, J. Wagner, Union County.

225 Mrs Elizabeth Kulp, Pennsylvania and New Jersey, Church and Town Records, 1708-1985 about Mrs Elizabeth Culp. Source Citation: Historical Society of Pennsylvania; Historic Pennsylvania Church and Town Records; Reel: 234.

226 Peter Batdorf, Descendants of Peter Batdorf, Evelyn S. Hartman.

227 Valentine Welker, Direct Descendants of Valentine (Welcher) Welker, Evelyn S. Hartman.

228 Dauphin County Names, Data p, Robert M Howard, www://genealogy.lv/howard/.

229 Welker family information, Roger Cramer, rogercubs@aol.com.

230 John Welker, U.S., Find A Grave Index, 1600s-Current, Ancestry.com. U.S., Find A Grave Index, 1600s-Current [database on-line]. Provo, UT, USA: Ancestry.com Operations, Inc., 012. Original data: Find A Grave. Find A Grave. http://www.findagrave.com/cgi-bin/fg.cgi.

231 Welker Family, Gratz History, p 450-455.

232 Pats Family, Pat Scott, pat.scott@comcast.net, awt.ancestry.com.

233 Elizabeth Messerschmidt, Pennsylvania Church Records - Adams, Berks, and Lancaster Counties, 1729-1881 about Elizabeth Messerschmidt.

234 Peters Research, Michael McCormick, Enduring Legacy, Gardners, PA, Feb 2009.

235 Peters household, 1850 United States Federal Census, Union, PA, 288, ancestry.com & Microfilm, PA State Library, Hbg, PA.

236 Maria Peters, Death notice, Lewisburg Chronicle, Oct. 1852 c/o Union County Historical Society, Maggie Miller, hstorici@ptd.net.

237 Jacob Wert, Wert family, Onetree, ancestry.com.

238 Elizabeth Wert death record, Extract from County Death records, 1893-1906.

239 Shoop family information, Are you my cousin, Harold Ward, haroldw1@juno.com, awt.ancestry.com.

240 Shoop family information, Northumberland Co County, PA 1777-1865, Stone Valley Lutheran, www.ancestry.com.

241 Johannes Schup, Stone Valley Cemetery, Robert Straub, Dalmatia, PA, Section A, Row 16, Grave 30.

242 Wert Family, Jonathan Wert, www.mdi-wert.com.

243 Sarah Wertz, David C Paul, Owner: dcpnascar7781, ancestry.com.

244 The Lunnys, William Lunny, rlunny@msn.com, awt.ancestry.com.

245 Frank Rowe, FHL, Pedigree chart, www.familysearch.org.

246 William Rowe, Family Data Collection, Individual Records, www.ancestry.com, Edmund West, comp.

247 William Rowe, Rowe family, Onetree, ancestry.com.

248 William Rowe, Descendants of Frank (Rau) Rowe, Evelyn S. Hartman.

249 Johann Wilhelm Frantz, Descendants of Johann Wilhelm Frantz, Evelyn S. Hartman.

250 Adam Frantz, Frantz family, Onetree, ancestry.com.

251 Gieseman family information, Mary Smith.

252 Franz-Gieseman marriage record, October 1811, source unknown.

253 Susanna Franz, St. John's Congr., 17 feb 1826, Mifflin, Dauphin Co, PA, Gert, gert@foothill.net.

254 Franz-Gieseman marriage record, October 1811, Lykens Valley lower church (David's Reformed) Millersburg, Upper Paxton, Dauphin Co, 1774-1844.

255 Susanna Franz, St. John's Congr.17 feb 1826, Mifflin, Dauphin Co, PA, Gert Mysliwski, gert@foothill.net.

256 Michael Lyman, David R. Layman, Biography, source unknown.

257 Lehman-Klein marriage record, June 28, 1818, Church Book records 4.

258 Lehman-Klein marriage record, Marriages at Trinity Lutheran Church, Lancaster Co, PA, Joan E. Kahler, Charles.Kahler@worldnet.att.net.

259 David R. Layman, Biography, source unknown.

260 John Rieman, 1850 United States Federal Census, Year: 1850; Census Place: York South Ward, York, Pennsylvania; Roll: M432_839; Page: 74B; Image: 722.

261 Michael Oberland, 1798, #3, York County Births 1730-1900, Humphrey, Gert Mysliwski,gert@foothill.net.

262 Michael Oberland, St. Matthews Lutheran Church records, Hanover, PA, Helda Kline.

263 Warner family information, JWerner.txt, Don Varner, DRVarner@aol.com.

264 Maria Catharina Werner, baptismal record, St Jacobs Lutheran Church, Vicki Kessler, Secretary, saintjacobslutheranchurch@msn.com.

265 Gipe Family of Chanceford Twp., York Co, 1997, Harry A. Diehl, p 1-5.266 William Anderson, FHL, Pedigree chart, www.familysearch.com.

267 William Anderson, February, 1840, Abstracts of Wills, Chapman, PA.

268 Anderson family information, Bob Anderson, PA, rmorris@ptd.net.

269 Anderson family information, Lisa betts, betts@sprintmail.com.

270 Catharina Arnold, Reformed Church Records in Eastern Pennsylvania, Copied by Dr. William J. Hinke, Church Records of Zion's or Stone Valley Lutheran and Reformed Church, http://www.mahantongo.org.

271 Arnold family, FHL, Pedigree Chart, Ancestral File, www.familysearch.org.

272 Bordner family information, Roger Cramer, rogercubs@aol.com.

273 Descendants of Philip Jacob Bortner, John Getz, jgetz@iu.net.

274 Children of Johann Michael Emerich, The Bordner & Burtner Families, H.W. Bordner, Washington DC, 1967, p 10.

275 Emerick family information, Ancestors & Descendants of Johann Michael Emerich of New York 1709-1979, O. S. Emrich, Ann Fenley, Dayton, OH.

276 Gaugler family information, author unknown.

277 Gaugler Notes, Dauphin County Courthouse, Ronald W. Huber, Salfordsville, PA, 1978.

278 Mary Gaugler, Mount Zion United Brethren Church Cemetery, Snyder Co, PA, Shaffer & Arnold, 1904, www.rootsweb.com.

279 Wriah Kelly, Pennsylvania, Death Certificates, 1906-1963 [database on-line]. Provo, UT, USA: Ancestry.com Operations, Inc., 2014.

280 Wm Kelly, Mount Zion United Brethren Church Cemetery, Snyder Co, PA, Shaffer & Arnold, 1904, www.rootsweb.com.

281 Shaffer family information, Debra Kassing, dk2_inc@msn.com.

282 Elizabeth Kelly, Mount Zion United Brethren Church Cemetery, Snyder Co, PA, Shaffer & Arnold, 1904, www.rootsweb.com.

283 Keefer, Kiefer file, Northumberland Co County Historical Society, Sunbury, PA.

284 My Family, Dillon, Kelly, Peterson, etc., Clint Dillon, treegnome@msn.com, awt.ancestry.com.

285 Lycoming County PA & Related Families, Harold E. Bower, Jr., harold.bower@usa.com, awt.ancestry.com.

286 Keefer Book, Pedigree Chart, The Family of Frederick Kieffer, Chapter V, p 1318, E.G. Keefer, 1997.

287 David Kieffer, Union Cemetery Co, Delongs Reformed Church records, Bowers, PA.

288 Peter Kieffer Sr, NSSAR Ecord copy, SAR application, Samuel L Savidge, Northumberland, PA, Nat # 114561, State #8464, Jun 1978.

289 Daniel Keefer, Probate files, 1862, Northumberland County Courthouse, Reg of Wills, Sunbury, Bk 6, p170, PA, Robyn Jackson, genealogylover@msn.com, 2008.

290 John Conrad Bucher, Bucher family, Onetree, ancestry.com.

291 Livezly-Culen marriage record, Gloria Dei Church, 916 S Swanson, Philadelphia, PA 19147, bk 18, p 6.

292 History of Pennsylvania volunteers, 1861-5; prepared in compliance with acts of the legislature, by Samuel P. Bates. Collection: Making of America Books History of Pennsylvania volunteers, 1861-5; prepared in compliance with acts of the legislature, by Samuel P. Bates, 1827-1902.

293 http://155thpa.tripod.com/id2.html - see pictures of the uniforms here.

294 http://civilwar.gratzpa.org/2011/01/tower-city-porter-township-centennial-civil-war-veterans-list/

295 http://civilwar.gratzpa.org/2012/01/alexander-f-thompson-senator-and-attorney/

296 http://civilwar.gratzpa.org/2012/01/alexander-f-thompson-senator-and-attorney/; http://www.findagrave.com/cgi-bin/fg.cgi?page=gr&GRid=117381891

297 http://civilwar.gratzpa.org/2012/01/alexander-f-thompson-senator-and-attorney/

298 http://civilwar.gratzpa.org/2012/04/2012-additions-to-civil-war-veterans-list-g-to-i/

299 http://civilwar.gratzpa.org/veterans/Charles McKean, "Edinburgh: 3. 1750 Onwards" in: The Oxford Companion to Scottish History, Edited by Michael Lynch, OUP, 2007

300 http://coalregionhistorychronicles.blogspot.com/2008/09/explosion-at-york-farm-colliery.html

301 http://en.wikipedia.org/wiki/Ludlow_Massacre

302 http://explorepahistory.com/story.php?storyId=1-9-4

303 http://files.usgwarchives.net/pa/schuylkill/history/local/munsell/hist0012.txt

304 http://files.usgwarchives.net/pa/schuylkill/military/civilwar/captured.txt

305 http://historynewsnetwork.org/article/623

306 http://quod.lib.umich.edu/m/moa/aby3439.0004.001/818?page=root;sid=41cea510eb7635c5b3e50413737b17fb; size=100;view=image;q1=One+Hundred+And+Fifty-Fifth+Regiment

307 http://quod.lib.umich.edu/m/moa/aby3439.0004.001/818?page=root;sid=41cea510eb7635c5b3e50413737b17fb; size=100;view=image;q1=One+Hundred+And+Fifty-Fifth+Regiment History of Pennsylvania volunteers, 1861-5; prepared in compliance with acts of the legislature, by Samuel P. Bates. Collection: Making of America Books http://quod.lib.umich.edu/m/moa/aby3439.0004.001/818?page=root;sid=41cea510eb7635c5b3e50413737b17fb;size=100;view=i mage;q1=One+Hundred+And+Fifty-Fifth+Regiment.

308 http://ultimatehistoryproject.com/before-the-whiteout-wedding-dresses-and-grooms-outfits.html

309 http://usminedisasters.com/Mine_Disasters/search_Coal_state.asp?ACC_STATE_NAME=Pennsylvania&x= 11&y=15

310 http://www.civilwar.org/education/history/warfare-and-logistics/warfare/richmond.html

311 http://www.civilwararchive.com/Unreghst/unpacav1.htm#9th

312 http://www.dailykos.com/story/2013/09/22/1211516/-Sweet-Home-Schuylkill-County-The-PA-Anthracite-coal-region-1790-1917#

313 http://www.dailykos.com/story/2013/09/23/1211516/-Sweet-Home-Schuylkill-County-The-PA-Anthracite-coal-region-1790-1917.

314 http://www.digitalarchives.state.pa.us/archive.asp?view=ArchiveItems&ArchiveID=17&FL=G&FID= 1194432&LID=1194481

315 http://www.ebooksread.com/authors-eng/jm-runk--company/commemorative-biographical-encyclopedia-of-dauphin-county-pennsylvania--contai-urm/page-198-commemorative-biographical-encyclopedia-of-dauphin-county-pennsylvania--contai-urm.shtml

316 http://www.findagrave.com/cgi-bin/fg.cgi?page=gr&GRid=62785330

317 http://www.lancasteratwar.com/2011/12/here-comes-cavalry-part-ii-lochiel.html

318 http://www.measuringworth.com/uscompare

319 http://www.measuringworth.com/uscompare/relativevalue.php

320 http://www.pacivilwar.com/regiment/155th.html

321 http://www.pacivilwar.com/regiment/191st.html

322 http://www.pagenweb.org/~schuylkill/castle/castle19.jpg

323 http://www.rootsweb.ancestry.com/~padauph2/lykinsnews.html

324 http://zouavedatabase.weebly.com/civil-war-zouave-unit-master-list.html

325 https://archive.org/stream/troopsundercomma01harr/troopsundercomma01harr_djvu.txt

326 https://books.google.com/books?id=eCk_AQAAMAAJ&pg=PA159&lpg=PA159&dq=Bast+%26+Thompson +Schuylkill+county+mines&source=bl&ots=CWTape7T1m&sig=Qm3SW59QO91reKpIIeicM0cI0UU&hl=en&sa=X&ei=9Jj-VPrtCMu0ggTCrYHgDA&ved=0CC4Q6AEwAw#v=onepage&q=Bast%20%26%Thompson%20 Schuylkill%20county%20mines&f=false

327 https://books.google.com/books?id=j3NWAAAAYAAJ&pg=PA1080&lpg=PA1080&dq=solomon+ updegrove+d.+1864+georgia&source=bl&ots=8iZFQh28Zi&sig=XR_F0FkDZ9F8_9Bp206AZktxp2I&hl=en&sa=X&ved=0CB 8Q6AEwAGoVChMIhbGV5_G7xwIVDOCACh138gBg#v=onepage&q=solomon%20updegrove%20d.%201864%20georgia&f =false; http://www.findagrave.com/cgi-bin/fg.cgi?page=gr&GRid=84377395

328https://books.google.com/books?id=MTTAAAAIAAJ&pg=PA179&dq=%22daniel+updegrove%22&hl=en&sa=X&ved=0CC4Q6AEwA2oVChMI_67k2MKnxwIVy6CACh1IaQDu#v=onepage&q=daniel%20updegrove&f=false, Weekly Notes of Cases Argued and Determined in the Supreme Court ..., Volume 20

329 https://books.google.com/books?id=rRwQAAAAYAAJ&pg=PA308&lpg=PA308&dq=Captain+John+McMillan%E2%80%99s+company,+Colonel+Fenton%E2%80%99s+regiment,+of+the+Pennsylvania+Militia&source=bl&ots=YpSCK5C7sj&sig=hKIwaYSwScmid-HNUo_kavB2_EE&hl=en&sa=X&ei=_cpfVfnLMczBsAXt-YAI&ved=0CDIQ6AEwBA#v=onepage&q=Captain%20John%20McMillan%E2%80%99s%20company%2C%20Colonel%20Fenton%E2%80%99s%20regiment%2C%20of%20the%20Pennsylvania%20Militia&f=false

330 https://books.google.com/books?id=xr-rrOqOPysC&pg=PA553&lpg=PA553&dq=Lochiel+Cavalry+and+libby+prison&source=bl&ots=31SzP5eI6A&sig=g46Cqj-M4kAZOwYpx5fCh84j6Oo&hl=en&sa=X&ved=0CEMQ6AEwBmoVChMIgr6vufqnxwIVw4MNCh0nyA2A#v=onepage&q=Lochiel%20&f=false A Scout to East Tennessee by the Lochiel Cavalry. Anecdotes, Poetry, and Incidents of the War: North and South: 1860-1865, By Frank Moore

331 https://books.google.com/books?id=zagAAAAYAAJ&printsec=frontcover&source=gbs_ge_summary_r&cad=0#v=onepage&q=hensel&f=false; After the Reserves: An Unofficial History of the 190th and 191st Pennsylvania Volunteer Infantry Regiments, June 1, 1864 through June 28, 1865

332 http://www.pareserves.com/files/pdf_files/AFTER%20THE%20RESERVES.PDF Under the Maltese Cross (1910)

333 https://en.wikipedia.org/wiki/Libby_Prison_Escape

334 https://www.lycoming.edu/umarch/chronicles/2011/2Evangelical.pdf

335 Luther Reily Kelker, History of Dauphin County, Pennsylvania: With Genealogical Memoirs, Volumes 1-2, p. 1080

336 Schuylkill County Firefighting by Michael R. Glore and Michael J. Kitsock. Arcadia Publishing, 2010.

337 The West Schuylkill Herald, Jan 3, 1901, Jeffrey A. Brown, ntrprz@dmv.com

338 Collection: Making of America Books

339 Tower City, Porter Township Centennial book, 1868-1968, Records of Jim Thompson, jbthompson@compuserve.com

340 http://archive.org/stream/lykenswilliamsva00barr/lykenswilliamsva00barr_djvu.txt

341 http://archive.org/stream/lykenswilliamsva00barr/lykenswilliamsva00barr_djvu.txt Harrisburg Patriot Sept. 7, 1891

342 http://archive.org/stream/lykenswilliamsva00barr/lykenswilliamsva00barr_djvu.txt Lykens-Williams Valley directory and pictorial review Map population density of the United States from the 1810 census www.wfu.edu Lykens-Williams Valley directory and pictorial review Annals of Buffalo Valley, Pennsylvania, 1755-1855, Linn, John Blair

343 http://explorepahistory.com/story.php?storyId=1-9-E&chapter=1 (Dauphin from state data)

344 http://www.carnegielibrary.org/research/ Lykens-Williams Valley history - directory and pictorial review

345 http://www.wtwp.org/ Harrisburg Patriot, January 18, 1906 Harrisburg Patriot,

346 http://www.dcnr.state.pa.us/cs/groups/public/documents/document/dcnr_009325.pdf

347 http://www.dcnr.state.pa.us/cs/groups/public/documents/document/dcnr_009325.pdf

348 http://www.dol.gov/dol/aboutdol/history/coalstrike.htm

349 http://www.familysearch.org Harrisburg Patriot, August 23, 1917 Lykens - Williams Valley History Directory J. Allen Barrett ancestry.com

350 http://www.msha.gov/District/Dist_01/History/history.htm

351 http://www.pbs.org/wned/war-of-1812/timeline/ Lykens-Williams Valley history,

352 http://www.portal.state.pa.us/portal/server.pt/community/events/4279/

353 http://www.reviewhttp://archive.org/stream/lykenswilliamsva00barr/lykenswilliamsva00barr_djvu.txt

354 http://www.unioncountyhistoricalsociety.orgAnnals of Buffalo Valley, Pennsylvania, 1755-1855 Linn, John Blair 1850 United States Census Annals of Buffalo Valley, Pennsylvania, 1755-1855 Linn, John Blair Lykens-Williams Valley history - directory and pictorial

355 Brief history of York County PA by George R. Powell; pg 28; copyright 1906

356 Catherine Duncan, Death certificate, Northumberland Co County Register of Wills, Sunbury, PA

357 Charley Duncan, Baptisms of Infants, Zion Evan Luth Register, 1851-1892, Sunbury, PA, p101

358 Charlotte Layman, Duncan family information, Stephanie Gormley

359 County of Northumberland Pennsylvania www.northumberlandco.org

360 David McCloud, Probate files, 1864, Northumberland County Courthouse, Reg of Wills, Sunbury, Bk 5, p261, PA

361 David R. Layman, Biography, source unknown

361 Donkert household, 1880 United States Census, Northumberland Co, PA, ancestry.com & Microfilm, PA State Library, Hbg, PA

363 Duncan death certificate, #0030852, #90924, Northumberland Co, PA, Department of Vital records, New Castle, PA

364 Duncan family information, 1870 United States Census, York Co, PA, Roll M5931468, p 545, Image 700, ancestry.com & Microfilm, PA State Library, Hbg, PA

365 Duncan family information, Jack Lehman, North Charleston, SC

366 Duncan family information, Stephanie Gormley, PA, 1989

367 Duncan household, 1900 United States Census, microfilm image, PA State Library. Died Sunbury, PA,

368 Duncan household, 1900 United States Census, microfilm image, PA State Library

369 Duncan household, 1910 United States Census, Northumberland Co, PA, ED 0118, Visit 0155, ancestry.com & Microfilm, PA State Library, Hbg, PA

370 Duncan-Layman marriage record, #8855, Northumberland Co, PA, 1899, Northumberland Co County Register of Wills, Sunbury, PA

371 Duncan-Layman marriage record, April 20, 1899, Edward C. Eisley

372 Dungan household, 1870 United States Census, Northumberland Co, PA, ancestry.com & Microfilm, PA State Library, Hbg, PA

373 Dungard household, 1870 United States Census, Northumberland Co, PA, ancestry.com & Microfilm, PA State Library, Hbg, PA

374 ED 134, Image 0913, ancestry.com & Microfilm, PA State Library, Hbg, PA

375 Elmira Layman, Bethel ME Cemetery, p 151, Jerome K. Hively, Brogue, PA

376 en.wikipedia.org/wiki/Airville%2C_Pennsylvania

377 files.usgwarchives.net/pa/northumberland/areahistory/bell0011.txt   153 Bell's History of Northumberland County Pennsylvania transcribed by Tony Rebuck for use in USGenWeb Archives pages 309 – 311 & 705 –   707 378 http://en.wikipedia.org"Vikings" and "Scottish trades in early modern era" http://www.portal.state.pa.us/ Pennsylvania history – Independence to Civil War

379 First Electric Light Historical Marker, www.explorepahistory.com/hmarker.php?markerId=1-A-399

380 Hannah Artilla Duncan, Baptisms of Infants, Zion Evan Luth Register, 1851-1892, Sunbury, PA, p94

381 Hawkins household, 1900 United States Census, Northumberland Co, PA, ancestry.com & Microfilm, PA State Library, Hbg, PA.

382 Hawkins household, 1920 United States Census, Cook, IL, ancestry.com & Microfilm, PA State Library, Hbg, PA

383 History of Pennsylvania agriculture   http://www.portal.state.pa.us

384 How the Homestead Act Transformed America, www.smithsonianmag.com/history-archaeology/How-the-Homestead-Act-Transformed-America.html

385 http://books.google.com/books?id=X6fhAAAAMAAJ&pg=PA542&lpg=PA542&dq= W.+C.+Calhoun+1901+copper+mine+swindler&sourc e=bl&ots=V-k0i6JsDx&sig=3BQzIxEdNPol7CaiZS2G3kDiW6g&hl=en&sa=X&ei=ZceEUrLQOqnhiAKNmIHYCg&ved=0CCwQ6AEwA Q#v=onepage&q=W.%20C.%2cCalhoun%201901%20copper%20mine%20swindler&f=false, The Copper Handbook, Volumes 8, By Horace Jared Stevens, Walter Harvey Weed,

386 http://en.wikipedia.org/ History of Elizabethtown PA

387 http://en.wikipedia.org/Flatboats http://www.distancebetweencities.net/ http://www.houseofnames.com

388 http://en.wikipedia.org/William McKinley 200 http://www.yorkblog.com/ York Furnace Bridge

389 http://files.usgwarchives.net/pa/york/history/gibson/chanceford-twp.txt The Township of Chanceford, York County, PA, B. F. Porter, M. D., 1886 -

390 http://liveauctions.holabirdamericana.com/CO-Copperfield-Fremont-County-1900-Colorado-Copper-Mining-Company-Stock-Certificate-Fenske-C_i10680523 Colorado Copper Mining Co.

391 http://sharing.ancestry.com/3045477?h=16e789

392 http://www.measuringworth.com/ppowerus/, Measuringworth.com

393 http://www.cityofsunbury.com/ Blacksmithing History 1 - http://www.appaltree.net/aba/hist1.htm

394 http://www.cyberdriveillinois.com/GenealogyMWeb/ODPHdeathsearch

395 http://www.cyberdriveillinois.com/GenealogyMWeb/ODPHdeathsearch.1916-

396 http://www.donicht.de/lutheraner.htm Old Lutheran immigration fever,

397 http://www.gdhspa.org/Dover/flood%20of%201884.htm The Inundation of York, Penna: A Graphic Description of the Great Flood: with an Account of the Violent Rain Storm of June 25, 1884 (Google eBook) - F. L. Spangler, York Daily Printing House, 1884 Flood of 1884

398 http://www.gendisasters.com/data1/ny/earthquakes/eastcoast-earthquake-aug1884.htm 1884 August Earthquake 399 http://www.genealogy.com/24_land.html Revolutionary War Bounty Land Grants -

400 http://www.mahantongo.org/mmhps/stoneval.htm a link from the Northumberland Historical Society found on the City of Sunbury website

401 http://www.mahantongo.org/mmhps/stoneval.htm Zion Stone Valley Church

402 http://www.mayoclinic.com Symptoms of nephritis

403 http://www.healthline.com, Symptoms of cystitis

404 http://www.phmc.state.pa.us Pennsylvania Historical Museum Commission

405 http://www.phmc.state.pa.us/ - Lancaster County http://www.padutchcountry.com Marietta, Lancaster Co. PA

406 http://www.portal.state.pa.us Pennsylvania Historical & Museum Commission

407 http://www.portal.state.pa.us/portal/server.pt/community/overview_of_pennsylvania_history/4281 Pennsylvania Historic & Museum Commission -

408http://www.portal.state.pa.us/portal/server.pt/community/pennsylvania%27s_agricultural_history/2584 Pennsylvania Historic & Museum Commission,

409 http://www.wlsessays.net/files/WesterhausEmigrations.pdf The Confessional Lutheran Emigrations from Prussia and Saxony Around 1839,

410 http://www.yorkblog.com/How did they get across the wide Susquehanna when there were no bridges?

411 http://yorkcountypa.gov/History York County PA http://web.archive.org/ — Agriculture in Lancaster PA

Jefferson Copper Mining Co. Colorado - Scripopholy.com

412 http://scripophily.net/jecomicoco19.html

413 John Reiman, York Co, PA Will index, Gert Mysliwski, gert@foothill.net. http://en.wikipedia.org/ —Lancaster County

414 Joseph P Leyman, Evergreen Cemetery, Index files and lot lists, #5435, Lot SG 157, Maple Gr Pt 6, vault 5/9/box, permit #4976, Chicago, IL

415 Joseph Pierce Layman, death record, Illinois Statewide Death Index, 1916-

416 Joseph Pierce Layman, State of IL, Dept of Public Health, DVS, Reg #4976, Primary Dt #3104, Cook, IL, Feb 1924.

417 Klein household, 1820 United States Census, Lancaster Co, PA, ancestry.com & Microfilm, PA State Library, Hbg, PA

418 Layman household, 1800 United States Census, Centre Co, PA, ancestry.com & Microfilm, PA State Library, Hbg, PA

419 Layman/Lehman family information, Files, NCHS, The Hunter House, Sunbury, PA

420 Laymen household, 1910 United States Census, Northumberland Co, PA, ED 0114, Visit 0085, ancestry.com & Microfilm, PA State Library, Hbg, PA

421 Laynon household, 1900 United States Census, Northumberland Co, PA, ancestry.com & Microfilm, PA State Library, Hbg, PA

422 Lehman-Klein marriage record, June 28, 1818, Church Book records 4

423 Lehman-Klein marriage record, Marriages at Trinity Lutheran Church, Lancaster Co, PA, Joan E. Kahler, Charles.Kahler@worldnet.att.net.

424 Lehman-Oberlander marriage, source unknown

425 Leyman family information, source unknown

426 Lottie Duncan, Pomfret Manor Cemetery, Sam Derr, Sunbury, PA, lot 130-B

427 Lottie V Willard death certificate, File #29987, Reg #19, #3505042, February 1936, Department of Vital Records, New Castle, PA

428 Lottie V. Willard, Lottie Duncan, Pomfret Manor Cemetery, Sam Derr, Sunbury, PA, lot 130-B

429 Lyman household, 1850 United States Census, York Co, PA, Roll M432-

430 Lyman household, 1860 United States Census, York Co, PA, ancestry.com & Microfilm, PA State Library, Hbg, PA

431 Lyman household, 1870 United States Census, York Co, PA, Roll M593 1468, p 545, Image 700, ancestry.com & Microfilm, PA, State Library, Hbg, PA

432 Lyman household, 1880 United States Census, York Co, PA, FHL 1255208, Film T9-1208, p 640D, www.familysearch.org

433 McCloud household, 1860 United States Census, Northumberland Co, PA, Series M653, Roll 1149, p 71, ancestry.com & Microfilm, PA State Library, Hbg, PA

434 McCloud household, 1870 United States Census, Northumberland Co, PA, ancestry.com & Microfilm, PA State Library, Hbg, PA

435 McCloud household, 1880 United States Census, Northumberland Co, PA, ancestry.com & Microfilm, PA State Library, Hbg, PA

436 McCloud-Frye, Marriage, Northumberland County, SS, #2856, Register & Recorder, Sunbury, PA, Oct 1890, Market St, Sunbury, PA.

437 McLeod household, 1850 United States Census, Northumberland Co, PA, ancestry.com & Microfilm, PA State Library, Hbg, PA

438 Melinda Duncan, Cemetery record, Apr 1933, A genealogists Guide to Burials in Northumberland Co, PA, Vol I, Meiser & Meiser, 1989

439 Michael Layman, Bethel ME Cemetery, p 151, Jerome K. Hively, Brogue, PA

440 National Heart and Lung Institute, What Causes Pneumonia? www.nhlbi.nih.gov

441 Layman Family information from Marc Thompson

442 Northumberland Co County Register of Wills

443 Oberlander household, 1830 United States Census, York Co, PA, ancestry.com & Microfilm, PA State Library, Hbg, PA

444 Oberlander household, 1840 United States Census, York Co, PA, ancestry.com & Microfilm, PA State Library, Hbg, PA

445 Oberlander household, 1850 United States Census, York Co, PA, Roll M432 839, p 839, ancestry.com & Microfilm, PA State Library, Hbg, PA

446 Oberlander household, 1860 United States Census, York Co, PA, ancestry.com & Microfilm, PA State Library, Hbg, PA

447 Oberlander household, 1870 United States Census, York Co, PA, ancestry.com & Microfilm, PA State Library, Hbg, PA

448 Oberlander household, 1880 United States Census, York Co, PA, FHL 1255207, Film T9-1207, p 599C, www.familysearch.org

449 Sarah Oberlander, Overlander-Kipe marriage record, #662-59, Calendar of Vital Records of the Counties of York & Adams

450 Pennsylvania in the Civil War www.wikipedia.org Brief history of York County PA by George R. Powell; pg 28; copyright 1906

451 Pennsylvania, 1851-92, Zion Evangelical Church, www.ancestry.com William Duncan, Baptisms of Infants, Zion Evan Luth Register, 1851-1892, Sunbury, PA, p41

452 Probate files, 1874, Rep 42, Bk 342, York County Archives, York, PA, Deborah Hershey, Elizabethtown, PA, Dec 2008

453 Rebecca Layman, Pomfret Manor Cemetery, Sam Derr, Sunbury, PA, lot 130-B

454 Rebecca Lehman (Layman) death certificate, #105066, Reg # 456, #3457529, November 1921, Department of Vital Records, New Castle, PA

455 Rieman household, 1820 United States Census, York Co, PA, ancestry.com & Microfilm, PA State Library, Hbg, PA

456 Robyn Jackson, genealogylover@msn.com, 2008

457 Sallie Duncan, Cemetery record, Apr 1933, A genealogists Guide to Burials in Northumberland Co, PA, Vol I, Meiser & Meiser, 1989

458 Sarah Duncan, Baptisms of Infants, Zion Evan Luth Register, 1851-1892, Sunbury, PA, p41

459 Sarah Oberlander, Probate files, 1874, Rep 42, York County Archives, York, PA, Deborah Hershey, Elizabethtown, PA, Dec 2008.

460 wiki.answers.com/Q/Why_did_people_leave_Germany_for_America_in_the_late_1800's?

461 Willard household, 1920 United States Census, Northumberland Co, PA, Roll T625 1611, p 7A, ED 134, Image 0913, ancestry.com & Microfilm, PA State Library, Hbg, PA

462 Willard household, 1930 United States Census, Northumberland Co, PA, Roll T626 2091, p 7A, ED 71, Image 0681, ancestry.com & Microfilm, PA State Library, Hbg, PA

463 William Duncan, Baptisms of Infants, Zion Evan Luth Register, 1851-1892, Sunbury, PA, p41

464 William Duncan, Northumberland Co County, Pennsylvania, 1851-92, Zion Evangelical Church, www.ancestry.com

465 William Duncan, Pomfret Manor Cemetery, Sam Derr, Sunbury, PA, lot 130-B

466 William Duncan, Pomfret Manor Cemetery, Sunbury, Northumberland Co, PA, NCHS, The Hunter House, Sunbury, PA

467 William Duncan, Probate files, July 1906, Northumberland County Courthouse, Reg of Wills, Bk 12, p424, Sunbury, PA, Robyn Jackson, genealogylover@msn.com, 2008

468 William Duncan, Probate files, July 1906, Northumberland County Courthouse, Reg of Wills, Bk 12, p424, Sunbury, PA, Robyn Jackson, genealogylover@msn.com, 2008.

469 Duncan family information, Jack Lehman, North Charleston, SC

470 Wm Duncan death certificate, #0030852, #90924, Northumberland Co, PA, Department of Vital records, New Castle, PA

471 Wm Duncan, Northumberland Co County Courthouse, Register of Wills, 11-27-1901

472 http://cigarhistory.info/Cigar_History/History_1878-1915.html

473 http://en.wikipedia.org/wiki/Dyeing

474 http://en.wikipedia.org/wiki/History_of_cancer

475 http://en.wikipedia.org/wiki/Pennsylvania

476 http://en.wikipedia.org/wiki/Pennsylvania_Canal

477 http://en.wikipedia.org/wiki/Samuel_Gompers

478 http://en.wikipedia.org/wiki/Snyder_County,_Pennsylvania

479 http://explorepahistory.com/story.php?storyId=1-9-10

480 http://explorepahistory.com/story.php?storyId=1-9-21

481 http://www.allentownsd.org/Page/16

482 http://www.ancestry.com/name-origin?surname=bordner

483 http://www.ancestry.com/name-origin?surname=gaugler

484 http://www.phme.state.pa.us/bhp/AQL/context/Central_Limestone_Valleys.pdf

485 http://en.wikipedia.org/wiki/Pennsylvania_Lumber_Museum

486 http://www.princeton.edu/history/people/display_person.xml?netid=hartog&interview=yes

487 http://www.prrths.com

488 http://www.shmoop.com/1920s/economy.html

489 http://www.wiley.com/legacy/products/subject/business/forbes/ford.html

490 http://en.wikipedia.org/wiki/Rural_electrification#United_States

491 http://zerbetownship.org/history.asp

492 http://en.wikipedia.org/wiki/Ashland,_Pennsylvania

493 http://en.wikipedia.org/wiki/Brakeman

494 http://en.wikipedia.org/wiki/Federal_Employers_Liability_Act

495 http://www.pinegrovetownship.com/History.html

496 http://www.questia.com/library/history/social-history/women-in-19th-century-america

497 http://www.answers.com/topic/sewing-machine

498 http://www.answers.com/topic/clothing-industry

499 http://www.nps.gov/civilwar/search-regiments-detail.htm?regiment_id=UPA0172RIX 32

500 http://en.wikipedia.org/wiki/Pennsylvania_in_the_American_Civil_War

501 http://www.etymonline.com/cw/draft.htm

502 http://en.wikipedia.org/wiki/Militia_%28United_States%29#Civil_War

503 http://en.wikipedia.org/wiki/Peninsula_Campaign

504 http://en.wikipedia.org/wiki/History_of_education_in_the_United_States#One-room_schoolhouses

505 http://en.wikipedia.org/wiki/Port_Trevorton,_Pennsylvania

506 http://www.portal.state.pa.us/portal/server.pt/community/pennsylvania%27s_agricultural_history/2584

507 http://www.portal.state.pa.us/portal/server.pt/community/pennsylvania%27s_agricultural_history/2584/
North_and_West_Branch.pdf

508 http://relationships.blurtit.com/1647575/what-was-the-average-family-size-in-the-19th-century

509 http://en.wikipedia.org/wiki/Pennsylvania_in_the_American_Civil_War

510 http://en.wikipedia.org/wiki/Shamokin_%28village%29

511 http://en.wikipedia.org/wiki/Sunbury,_Pennsylvania

512 http://en.wikipedia.org/wiki/Pennsylvania_Canal

513 http://en.wikipedia.org/wiki/File:Pennsylvania_canals.png

514 http://en.wikipedia.org/wiki/Main_Line_of_Public_Works

515 http://en.wikipedia.org/wiki/Pennsylvania_Railroad

516 http://explorepahistory.com/story.php?storyId=1-9-10

517 http://hatbox.com/hat-history.cfm 50 http://en.wikipedia.org/wiki/Mad_hatter_disease

518 http://en.wikipedia.org/wiki/History_of_the_Ursulines_in_New_Orleans

519 http://en.wikipedia.org/wiki/Ashland,_Pennsylvania

520 http://www.rootsweb.ancestry.com/~wibrown/naming.htm

521 http://www.behindthename.com

SOURCES B

1 Eddie Mazo, December 1997, GA, Social Security Death Index, www.ancestry.com.

2 Eddie Mazo, Certificate of Death, #054861, Sumter, GA, State Registrar, Atlanta, GA.

3 Delored Curry death certificate, #124-544, February, 1948, Chatham, GA, State Office of Vital Records.

4 Kressie Joe Curry, Birth register, no name, 2-23-1948, Vital records, Chatham Co Health Dept, PO Box 14257, Savannah, GA.

5 Eddie Mazo, December 1997, GA, Social Security Death Index, www.ancestry.com.

6 Ned Mason, Certificate of Death, #054861, Sumter, GA, State Registrar, Atlanta, GA.

7 Mr. Eddie Mazo, Sect I, # 682, United States Dept. of the Interior, NSP, Andersonville National Historical Site, Andersonville, GA, Gerry Allen.

8 Jones household, 1920 United States Federal Census, Fulton, GA, ancestry.com &Microfilm, PA State Library, Hbg, PA.

9 Bank household, 1900 United States Census, Jefferson, AL, ancestry.com & Microfilm, PA State Library, Hbg, PA.

10 Eddie Mazo, United States WW II Army Enlistment Records, 1938-1946, NARA, www.ancestry.com.

11 Mr. Eddie Mazo, United States Dept. of the Interior, NSP, Andersonville National Historical Site, Andersonville, GA, Gerry Allen.

12 Eddie Mazo, United States World War II Army Enlistment Records, 1938-1946, NARA,www.ancestry.com.

13 Delores Curry death certificate, #124-544, February, 1948, Chatham, GA, State Office of Vital Records.

14 Mack Mason, Social Security numident record, application for SS-5, SSA, Nov 2006, Baltimore, MD.

15 Mack Mason death certificate, #24230, #1271, September 1962, Chatham, GA, State Office of VitalRecords.

16 Mack Mason Sr. death certificate, #24230, September 1962, Georgia Deaths 1919-98, Chatham, GA, www.ancestry.com, Kathryn Gordon Hamby.

17 Mack Mason Sr, GA Deaths, 1919-1998, #24230, www.ancestry.com.

18 Mason-Thompson marriage, State of Georgia, Washington Co, Marriage license, Washington Co Probate Court, 1902.

19 Mason household, 1910 United States Census, Jefferson, GA, ancestry.com & Microfilm, PA State Library, Hbg, PA.

20 Mason-Thompson marriage, Wash. Co Marriage Records, State of Georgia, Washington Co, Washington Co Probate Court, 1902, Book I, #519.

21 More household, 1900 United States Census, Washington Co, GA, ancestry.com &Microfilm, PA State Library, Hbg, PA.

22 Mason household, 1900 United States Census, Washington, GA, ancestry.com & Microfilm, PA State Library, Hbg, PA.

23 Mason household, 1920 United States Census, Jefferson, GA, www.ancestry.com, Kathryn Gordon Hamby.

24 Mason household, 1930 United States Census, Chatham Co, GA, ancestry.com & Microfilm, PA State Library, Hbg, PA.

25 Mason household, 1910 United States Census, Washington, GA, ancestry.com & Microfilm, PA State Library, Hbg, PA.

26 Mason household, 1930 United States Census, Chatham, GA, ancestry.com & Microfilm, PA State Library, Hbg, PA.

27 Mack Mason, 258-34-9996, SS-5, Application for SSA Number, Baltimore, MD.

28 Mack Mason, Jeff. Co Tax Digest 1907, Office of Probate Court, Jeff. Co, Courthouse, Louisville, GA.

29 Mason household, 1920 United States Census, Jefferson, GA, www.ancestry.com, Kathryn Gordon Hamby.

30 Mack Mason, September 1962, GA, Social Security Death Index, www.ancestry.com.

31 Shatteen household, 1900 United States Census, Washington Co, GA, ancestry.com &Microfilm, PA State Library, Hbg, PA.

32 Mason household, 1920 United States Census, Jefferson, GA, ancestry.com & Microfilm, PA State Library, Hbg, PA.

33 Mason household, 1920 United States Census, Chatham, GA, ancestry.com & Microfilm, PA State Library, Hbg, PA.

34 Robert Forsythe, SS-5 application, Application for SSN, Social Security Administration, 1945.

35 Forsyth-Curry marriage, Marriage License, State of GA, Chatham County, April 17, 1948.

36 Robert Forsythe, Robert Forsythe, United States Veterans Cemeteries, ca. 1800-2006,Tahoma Nat'l Cemetery, NCA, Provo, UT, myfamily.com, Inc., 2006, www.ancestry.com.

37 Robert Forsythe, Social Security Death Index, Provo, UT, 259-40-7505, www.ancestry.com.

38 Forsyth-Curry marriage, Marriage License, State of GA, Chatham County, April 17, 1948.

39 Cressie Curry, December 1998, issued PA, resided GA, Social Security Death Index, www.ancestry.com.

40 Forsyth-Curry marriage, Marriage License, State of GA, Chatham County, April 17, 1948. #059026, January 14, 1999, Georgia State Office of Vital Records, GA.

41 Cressie Curry death certificate, #059026, January 14, 1999, Georgia State Office of Vital Records, GA.

42 Robert Forsythe, Social Security numident record, application for SS-5, SSA, Nov 2006, Baltimore, MD.

43 Robert Forsythe, United States Veterans Cemeteries, ca. 1800-2006,Section J, Row B, site 85, Tahoma Nat'l Cemetery, NCA, Provo, UT, myfamily.com, Inc., 2006, www.ancestry.com.

44 Dunham household, 1930 United States Census, Chatham Co, GA, ancestry.com & Microfilm, PA State Library, Hbg, PA.

45 Robert Forsythe, United States Veterans Cemeteries, ca. 1800-2006,Tahoma Nat'l Cemetery, NCA, Provo, UT, myfamily.com, Inc., 2006, www.ancestry.com.

46 Nina Washington Forsythe, death certificate, Vitals Records, Ga Dept. of Public Health, 1944,Savannah, Chatham, GA.

47 Robert Forsythe, Tahoma National Cemetery Maple Valley, King County, Washington 18600 Southeast 240th St. Kent, WA 98042-4868.

48 Elizabeth Curry, Certificate of Death, Custodians #1401, October 1965, Vital records, Chatham Co Health Dept, PO Box 14257, Savannah, GA.

49 Cressie Mazo, SS-5, Application for SSN, 202-40-5156, March 1966, Social Security Administration.

50 Cressie Curry, December 10, 1998, GA, Social Security Death Index, www.ancestry.com.

51 Cressie Curry death certificate, #059026, January 14, 1999, Georgia State Office of Vital Records, GA and Cressie Curry, December 10, 1998, PA, Social Security Death Index, www.ancestry.com.

52 Aggie Palmer, Certificate of Death, Commonwealth of GA, State Board of Health, File#9966, Ivey, GA, Mar 1922.

53 Mason household, 1900 United States Census, Washington, GA, ancestry.com & Microfilm, PA State Library, Hbg, PA.

54 Mason household, 1870 United States Census, Washington, GA, ancestry.com & Microfilm,P A State Library, Hbg, PA.

55 Mason household, 1880 United States Census, Washington, GA, ancestry.com & Microfilm ,PA State Library, Hbg, PA.

56 Mason household, 1880 United States Census, Washington, GA, FHL 1254171, Film T9-0171, p 360B, www.familysearch.org.

57 Mason household, 1870 United States Census, Washington, GA, ancestry.com & Microfilm, PA State Library, Hbg, PA.

58 Edward Mason, 1888, Savannah, GA Directories, 1888-91, www.ancestry.com.

59 Mason household, 1870 United States Census, Washington, GA, Roll M593 182, p 261, Image199, ancestry.com & Microfilm, PA State Library, Hbg, PA.

60 Mason household, 1880 United States Census, Washington, GA, Roll T9-171, Film 1254171,p 360B, ED 129, Image 0102, ancestry.com & Microfilm, PA State Library, Hbg, PA.

61 Aggie Palmer, Certificate of Death, Commonwealth of GA, State Board of Health, File#9966, Ivey, GA, Mar 1922.

62 Mason-Wicker, Marriage license, State of Georgia, Washington County, Probate court, Sandersville, GA.

63 Mason-Clayton, Marriage license, State of Georgia, Washington County, Probate court, Sandersville, GA.

64 Thompson household, 1900 United States Census, Jefferson Co, GA, ancestry.com & Microfilm, PA State Library, Hbg, PA.

65 Thompson-Shatteen, marriage license, State of GA, Washington Co, Marriage records bk E, p 281, 1879-1885, Probate court of Washington Co, Sandersville, GA.

66 Annie Thompson, Savannah, Georgia, Cemetery and Burial Records, 1852-1939 about Annie Thompson.

67 Thompson household, 1880 United States Census, Washington Co, GA, ancestry.com &Microfilm, PA State Library, Hbg, PA.

68 Shatteen household, 1880 United States Census, Washington Co, GA, ancestry.com &Microfilm, PA State Library, Hbg, PA.

69 Forsythe household, 1900 United States Census, Duval, FL, ancestry.com & Microfilm, PA State Library, Hbg, PA.

70 Percy Forsythe, Chatham County, GA Probate court, Wills, Estates, Admins, etc., F778, Adm 1942.

71 Nina Washington Forsyth, Cemetery Record, City of Savannah, Cemeteries Dept., Savannah, GA c/o Jerry Flemming, Director of Cemeteries.

72 Nina Forsythe, Chatham County, GA Probate court, Wills, Estates, Admins, etc., F806, Adm 1944.

73 Forsyth household, 1910 United States Census, Duval, FL, ancestry.com & Microfilm, PA State Library, Hbg, PA.

74 Forsythe household, 1930 United States Census, Washington DC, ancestry.com & Microfilm, PA State Library, Hbg, PA.

75 Percy Campbell Forsythe, Naturalization index, NY Southern intentions, Percy Forsyth, 232663,398, fotenote.com.

76 Percy Campbell Forsythe, Mariners killed in WW2, City of Atlanta, www.usmm.org.

77 Percy C Forsythe, US Rosters of World War II Dead, 1939-1945, Merchant Marine, 196897, www.ancestry.com.

78 Robinson household, 1910 United States Census, Chatham Co, GA, ancestry.com & Microfilm,P A State Library, Hbg, PA.

79 Robinson household, 1920 United States Census, Chatham Co, GA, ancestry.com & Microfilm, PA State Library, Hbg, PA.

80 Freddie Curry, Certificate of Death, Custodians #1582, November 1964, Vital records, Chatham Co Health Dept, PO Box 14257, Savannah, GA.

81 Freddie Curry, Social Security numident record, application for SS-5, SSA, Nov 2006, Baltimore, MD.

82 Mack Mason, Chatham County Deaths, Wyonona Burgstiner, wburgstiner@yahoo.com.

83 Curry household, 1930 United States Census, Chatham, GA, T626, 2, 667, www.ancestry.com, GA-Census-lookup-d, Gina.

84 Curry-Brown marriage, Probate Court, Savannah, GA, p 307, bk 2R's, Sept. 17, 1928, application.

85 Elizabeth Curry, Chatham County Deaths, Wyonona Burgstiner, wburgstiner@yahoo.com.

86 No name Curry, Birth register, Dept. of Public Health, Chatam Co, GA, 2/15/07, Dunkin Curria & Betsy.

87 Freddie Curry, Lot 60, Sec B, Cemetery Record, City of Savannah, Cemeteries Dept., Savannah, GA c/o Jerry Flemming, Director of Cemeteries.

88 Curry household, United States Census, 1910, Chatham, GA, ancestry.com & Microfilm, PA State Library, Hbg, PA.

89 Curry household, United States Census, 1920, Chatham, GA, ancestry.com & Microfilm, PA State Library, Hbg, PA.

90 Curry household, 1930 United States Census, Chatham, GA, T626, 2, 667, ancestry.com &Microfilm, PA State Library, Hbg, PA.

91 Curry household, 1930 United States Census, Chatham, GA, ancestry.com & Microfilm, PA State Library, Hbg, PA.

92 Elizabeth Curry, Lot 60, Sec B, Cemetery Record, City of Savannah, Cemeteries Dept., Savannah, GA c/o Jerry Flemming, Director of Cemeteries.

93 Brown household, 1920 United States Census, Allendale Co, GA, ancestry.com & Microfilm ,PA State Library, Hbg, PA.

94 Mrs.. Elizabeth Curry, Savannah Morning News, Oct 17, 1965, Wyonona Burgstiner,wburgstiner@yahoo.com.

95 Neal household, 1880 United States Census, Washington, GA, ancestry.com & Microfilm, PA State Library, Hbg, PA.

96 Mason-Walker, Marriage license, State of Georgia, Washington County, Probate court, Sandersville, GA.

97 Mason-Adams, Marriage license, State of Georgia, Washington County, Probate court, Sandersville, GA.

98 Mason-Andrews, Marriage license, State of Georgia, Washington County, Probate court, Sandersville, GA.

99 Mason-Moffett, Marriage license, State of Georgia, Washington County, Probate court, Sandersville, GA.

100 Mason-Cumming, Marriage license, State of Georgia, Washington County, Probate court, Sandersville, GA.

101 Brown household, 1870 United States Census, Washington Co, GA, ancestry.com &Microfilm, PA State Library, Hbg, PA.

102 Thompson household, 1870 United States Census, Chatham Co, GA, ancestry.com & Microfilm, PA State Library, Hbg, PA.

103 Thomson household, 1880 US Federal Census, SD 3, ED 36, pg 11, Chatham, GA, p732,www.ancestry.com.

104 Thompson-Mason, Marriage license, State of Georgia, Washington County, Probate court, Sandersville, GA.

105 Thompson-Key, Marriage license, State of Georgia, Washington County, Probate court, Sandersville, GA.

106 Sallie Shateen, Cert of Death, File #26470, Reg #1516, 11/10/1927, GA Virtual
Vault,http://content.sos.state.ga.us/cdm4/gadeaths.php.

107 Sallie Shateen, Georgia Deaths, 1919-98, Chatham Co, GA, 1927, www.ancestry.com.

108 Shattine household, 1910 United States Census, Jefferson Co, GA, ancestry.com & Microfilm, PA State Library, Hbg, PA.

109 Shatteen household, 1920 United States Census, Chatham Co, GA, ancestry.com & Microfilm, PA State Library, Hbg, PA.

110 Shatteen-Hall, Marriage license, State of Georgia, Washington County, Probate court, Sandersville, GA.

111 Theophilus Forsythe, Cert of Death, File #05483, Reg #130, 5/23/1919, GA Virtual
Vault,http://content.sos.state.ga.us/cdm4/gadeaths.php.

112 Washington household, 1900 United States Census, Beaufort Co, SC, ancestry.com & Microfilm, PA State Library, Hbg, PA.

113 Joe Washington Jr, certificate of death, Beaufort, SC, 1922, South Carolina DHEC, Columbia, SC.

114 Joe Washington, Georgia, Deaths Index, 1914-1927 about Joe Washington, ancestry.com.

115 Robinson household, 1910 United States Census, Chatham, GA, ancestry.com & Microfilm, PA State Library, Hbg, PA.

116 Mary Washington, death record, Georgia Deaths, 1919-98, #7748, www.ancestry.com.

117 Washington household, 1870 United States Federal Census for Fortune Washington, ancestry.com.

118 Washington (Tennia) household, 1880 United States Census, Beaufort Co, SC, www,ancestry.com.

119 Washington (DC) household, 1880 United States Census, Beaufort Co, SC, www,ancestry.com.

120 Washington household, 1910 United States Census, Beaufort Co, SC, www,ancestry.com.

121 Washington household, 1900 United States Census, Beaufort Co, SC, www,ancestry.com.

122 Mary Washington, Laurel Grove Cemetery, Jerry Flemming, Director of Cemeteries, Savannah, GA.

123 Robinson household, 1880 United States Census, Beaufort Co, SC, ancestry.com & Microfilm, PA State Library, Hbg, PA.

124 Robinson household, 1920 United States Census, Chatham, GA, ancestry.com & Microfilm, PA State Library, Hbg, PA.

125 Dunham household, 1930 United States Census, Chatham, GA, ancestry.com & Microfilm, PA State Library, Hbg, PA.

126 Curry household, 1900 United States Census, Chatham, GA, ancestry.com & Microfilm, PA State Library, Hbg, PA.

127 Rosa Louise Curry, Certificate of Death, Commonwealth of GA, State Board of Health, File#13727, Chatham, GA, June 1922.

128 Henry Curry, Chatham County Deaths, Wyonona Burgstiner, wburgstiner@yahoo.com.

129 Duncan Curry, Death Register, June 1914, Chatham County Health Dept., Savannah, GA.

130 Bessie Curry, Georgia Deaths, 1919-98 about Bessie Curry, ancestry.com.

131 Duncan Curry, death certificate, Chatham, GA, Physician's Certificate of the Cause of death, June 1914, CCHD, Savannah, GA.

132 Curry household, United States Census, 1870, Beaufort Co, SC, ancestry.com & Microfilm, PA State Library, Hbg, PA.

133 Curry household, United States Census, 1880, Hampton, SC, ancestry.com & Microfilm, PA State Library, Hbg, PA.

134 Duncan Curry, Savannah, GA Directories, 1888-91, Provo, UT, myfamily.com, Inc.,2001, www.ancestry.com.

135 Colored boy, Birth Certificate, January 1909, Vital records, Chatham Co Health Dept, PO Box 14257, Savannah, GA.

136 Bessie Curry, Savannah, Georgia, Cemetery Burial Lot Cards, 1807-1995 about Bessie Curry, ancestry.com.

137 Alston household, 1880 United States Census, Hampton, SC, ancestry.com & Microfilm, PA State Library, Hbg, PA.

138 Curry household, 1940 United States Federal Census about Willy Curry, ancestry.com.

139 Joe Brown, U.S. World War 1 Draft Registration Cards, No 209, 39-1-3, Allendale, SC, 1942, www.ancestry.com.

140 Colored boy, birth certificate, April 1908, Chatham County Health Dept, Savannah, GA.

141 Joe Brown, Georgia Deaths, 1919-98 about Joe Brown, ancestry.com.

142 Nancy Brown, Georgia Deaths, 1919-98 about Nancy Brown, ancestry.com.

143 Brown household, 1900 United States Census, Barnwell Co, GA, ancestry.com & Microfilm, PA State Library, Hbg, PA.

144 Brown household, 1910 United States Census, Barnwell Co, GA, ancestry.com & Microfilm, PA State Library, Hbg, PA.

145 Brown household, United States Census, 1930, Chatham, GA, ancestry.com & Microfilm, PA State Library, Hbg, PA.

146 Brown household, 1940 United States Federal Census about Joe Brown, ancestry.com.

147 Frazier household, 1900 United States Census, Barnwell Co, GA, ancestry.com & Microfilm, PA State Library, Hbg, PA.

148 Frazier household, 1910 United States Census, Barnwell Co, GA, ancestry.com & Microfilm, PA State Library, Hbg, PA.

149 Houston household, 1870 United States Federal Census about Rhinor Brown, ancestry.com.

150 Robinson household, 1870 United States Census, Beaufort Co, SC, ancestry.com & Microfilm, PA State Library, Hbg, PA.

151 Robinson household, 1900 United States Census, Charleston, SC, www.amcestry.com.

152 Alston household, 1900 United States Census, Chatham, GA, www.amcestry.com.

153 Ben Alston, Savannah, Georgia Vital Records, 1803-1966 about Ben Alston, www.ancestry.com.

154 Ben Alston, Laurel Grove Cem listing, Jerry Flemming, Director of Cemetery, Savannah, GA,

Jerry_Flemming@SavannahGa.Gov.

155 Ben Alston, U.S., Find A Grave Index, 1700s-Current about Ben Alston, ancestry.com.

156 Allston household, 1870 United States Census, Beaufort Co, SC, ancestry.com & Microfilm, PA State Library, Hbg, PA.

157 Alston household, 1910 United States Census, Chatham, GA, ancestry.com & Microfilm, PA State Library, Hbg, PA.

158 Alston household, 1880 United States Census, Beaufort Co, SC, ancestry.com & Microfilm, PA State Library, Hbg, PA.

159 Benjamin Alston, Savannah, GA Directories, 1888-91, Provo, UT, myfamily.com, Inc.,2001, www.ancestry.com.

160 Alston household, 1880 United States Census, Lawnton, SC, ancestry.com & Microfilm, PA State Library, Hbg, PA.

161 Brown household, 1880 United States Federal Census about Joseph Brown, ancestry.com.

162 Glover household, 1880 United States Federal Census for Lena Glover, ancestry.com.

163 Samuel Frazier, Georgia Deaths, 1919-1998, ancestry.com.

164 Eva Frazier, Certificate of Death, January 1929, Chatham County Health Dept, State file #2, Savannah, GA.

165 Eva Frazier, Georgia Deaths, 1919-1998, ancestry.com.

166 Sam Frazier, death certificate, Chatham, GA, Local registrar's record of death, March 1928, CCHD, Savannah, GA.

167 Fraisier household, 1870 United States Census, Barnwell Co, GA, ancestry.com & Microfilm, PA State Library, Hbg, PA.

168 Fraser household, 1880 United States Census, Barnwell Co, GA, ancestry.com & Microfilm, PA State Library, Hbg, PA.

169 Frazier household, 1920 United States Census, Allendale Co, GA, ancestry.com & Microfilm, PA State Library, Hbg, PA.

170 Eva Frazier, Cemetery Record, City of Savannah, Cemeteries Dept., Savannah, GA c/o Jerry Flemming, Director of Cemeteries.

171 Thompson household, 1870 United States Census, Barnwell Co, GA, ancestry.com & Microfilm, PA State Library, Hbg, PA.

172 Brown household, 1870 United States Federal Census for David Brown, ancestry.com.

173 Brown household, 1880 United States Federal Census about David Brown, ancestry.com.

174 Hicks household, 1870 United States Federal Census for Milly Hay, ancestry.com.

175 Glover household, 1900 United States Federal Census about Lucia Glover, ancestr.com.

176 Dunbar household, 1900 United States Census, Barnwell Co, SC, ancestry.com & Microfilm, PA State Library, Hbg, PA.

177 Harley household, 1870 United States Federal Census for Lucia Harley, ancestry.com.

178 "I 'member well when the war was on." Enslavement & Emancipation during the Civil War: Selections from the WPA interviews of formerly enslaved African Americans, 1936-1938.

http://nationalhumanitiescenter.org/pds/maai/emancipation/text5/warslaveswpa.pdf

179 New Georgia Encyclopedia: Civil War in Georgia

http://www.georgiaencyclopedia.org/articles/history-archaeology/civil-war-georgia-overview

Sources for Mack Mason & Sarah A. Thompson Profile

Birth Dates and Identification of Parents For Both

Ancestry.com. "The Curry Family"

Information on Children's Names and Dates of Birth

Ancestry.com. "The Curry Family"

Ancestry.com: The U.S. Censuses: 1870 – 1940.

Reconstruction & the Effects of Union Military Occupation

New Georgia Encyclopedia, "Aftermath of the Civil War" and "The Freed Populace"

(http://www.georgiaencyclopedia.org/topics/civil-war-reconstruction-1861-1877)

Race Relations After Reconstruction - The Beginnings of Jim Crow

New Georgia Encyclopedia, "Late 19th Century, 1877 - 1900"

Our Documents.Gov, "Plessy v. Ferguson (1896)"

Black Past.org, "Plessy v. Ferguson (1896)"

Share-Cropping Following the Civil War

The History Channel, "Share Cropping" (http://www.history.com/topics/black-history/sharecropping).

A Georgia Sharecropper's Story of Forced Labor ca. 1900 (http://historymatters.gmu.edu/d/28)

Mason Family Movements and Employment

Ancestry.com: U.S. Census Reports for 1880 -

Sources for Edward Mazo & Delores Curry Profile

Birth Dates and Identification of Parents For Both

Ancestry.com. "The Curry Family"

Information on Children's Names and Dates of Birth

Ancestry.com. "The Curry Family"

Ancestry.com :The U.S. Censuses: 1880 – 1940.

Economics & Race Relations Following World War I

New Georgia Encyclopedia, "Jim Crow." and "The Great Depression & World War II"

(http://www.georgiaencyclopedia.org/topics/)

Ferris State University, Jim Crow Museum of Racist Memorabilia (www.ferris.edu/JIMCROW)

Constitutional Rights Foundation, A Brief History of Jim Crow (http://www.crf-usa.org/black-history-month/a-brief-history-of-jim-crow)

Eddie Mazo's Military History

National Archives and Records Administration. U.S. World War II Army Enlistment Records, 1938-1946; Citing the enlistment record of Eddie Mazo, 23 Nov 1945.

Sources for Edward "Ned" Mason & Rainey Brown Profile

Birth Dates and Identification of Parents For Both

Ancestry.com. "The Curry Family"

Information on Children's Names and Dates of Birth

Ancestry.com. "The Curry Family"

Ancestry.com :The U.S. Censuses: 1880 – 1900.

Statistics on Slaves in Washington County

Ancestry.com, 1860 Slave Schedule Addendum of the U.S. Census.

Conditions Under Slavery and Jobs Typically Performed by Slaves in Georgia

New Georgia Encyclopedia, "Slave Narratives": Slave Life in Georgia: A Narrative of the Life, Sufferings, and Escape of John Brown"

Born in Slavery: Slave Narratives from the Federal Writers' Project, 1936-1938: "Plantation Life" Interviews with Rachel Adams and Henry Bland (among others) former slaves in Georgia.

Race Relations During Reconstruction & the Beginnings of Jim Crow

New Georgia Encyclopedia, "Civil War & Reconstruction, 1861-1877"

 in Georgia" (http://www.georgiaencyclopedia.org/topics/civil-war-reconstruction-1861-1877)

Ferris State University, Jim Crow Museum of Racist Memorabilia (www.ferris.edu/JIMCROW)

Constitutional Rights Foundation, A Brief History of Jim Crow (http://www.crf-usa.org/black-history-month/a-brief-history-of-jim-crow)

Share-Cropping and Freed Slaves

The History Channel, "Share Cropping" (http://www.history.com/topics/black-history/sharecropping).

A Georgia Sharecropper's Story of Forced Labor ca. 1900 (http://historymatters.gmu.edu/d/28)

Sources for Robert J. Forsyth- Lucretia Jo Curry

Pre-World War II Economics

New Georgia Encyclopedia, Progressive Era to World War II.1900-1945, "The Great Depression"

(http://www.georgiaencyclopedia.org/articles/history-archaeology/great-depression)

Percy Campbell Forsythe's Death at the Hands of Nazis

U.S. Merchant Marine in World War II, "Merchant Mariners killed on U.S. operated ships during World War II,"

(http://www.usmm.org/killed/f.html)

Race Relations in Savannah Before and After World War II

A City of Divided Lives, Savannah Georgia (http://armstrongdigitalhistory.org/Exhibits/publicsegregationofsavannah/race-relations/)

Robert J. Forsythe's Incarceration

Ancestry.com. Georgia, Central Register of Convicts, 1817-1976; Felony Convict Record, State Board of Corrections, Atlanta, Georgia, "Robert J. Forsythe, File Number 22759, 2 February 1949".

Death and Burial Information for Both Subjects

Lucretia Jo Curry: http://www.findagrave.com/cgi-bin/fg.cgi?page=gr&GRid=14978077

Lucretia Jo Curry: Georgia Death Index, 1998

Robert J. Forsythe http://www.findagrave.com/cgi-bin/fg.cgi?page=gr&GRid=660776&ref=acom

Robert J. Forsythe: Social Security Death Index, 1935-2014

Sources for Percy Forsyth - Nina Washington Profile

Percy Campbell Forsythe's birth date was found on this WWI Draft Registration Card, which he signed: World War I Draft Registration Card, Serial Number 4179, Manhattan, New York City, New York, 12 September 1918.

Percy Campbell Forsythe's birth place and parents' names – "Bahamas Births, 1850-1891," database, FamilySearch (https://familysearch.org/): accessed 15 January 2016), Prescott Campbell Forsyth, 26 Jun 1879; citing Chapelry District of St. Agnes, Bahamas, reference 79; FHL microfilm 222,944.

[Note: Because of the difference in the first name, it was necessary to combine this record with the next one to be sure that Prescott and Percy were the same person. The marriage record described below named his parents and they were the same couple who registered the birth in this record.]

Percy Campbell Forsythe's First Marriage - New York, New York City Marriage Records, 1829-1940," database, FamilySearch (https://familysearch.org: accessed 15 January 2016), Persy Forsyth and Lulu Bachelor, 27 Sep 1915; citing Marriage, Manhattan, New York, New York, United States, New York City Municipal Archives, New York; FHL microfilm 1,614,227

Percy's Various Travels: Ancestry.com: Ships' Passengers and Crews to New York.

Ocean Steam Ship Company of Savannah – Information about this organization came from "The Ships List" http://www.theshipslist.com/ships/lines/savannah.shtml

Info on Bahamas Society – Caribbean Stratification http://www.capesociology.org/caribbean-stratification And Culture of Bahama Islands http://www.everyculture.com/A-Bo/Bahama-Islands.html

ABOUT THE AUTHOR

Marc D. Thompson delved into writing and researching at a very early age. As a youngster he wrote stories, poems, lyrics and articles. He continued putting pen to paper and studying medicine and genealogy throughout college, earning a B.S. degree from Moravian College. Marc has presented fitness and genealogical lectures and authored over 20 family histories for himself and his clients. His other fitness works include *Compendium of Virtual and Traditional Fitness, The Fitness Book of Lists, Virtual Personal Training Manual, Fitness Quotes of Humorous Inspiration* and *Poems of Eternal Moments*.

Marc wrote a monthly genealogy column for Atlantic Avenue Magazine and currently pens a monthly fitness and genealogy blog at www.marcdthompson.net. He is a member of the Association of Professional Genealogists and IDEAfit as well as the founder of a Pennsylvania Genealogy Society and currently organizing the South Palm Beach County Genealogical Society. Marc was the County Coordinator of the USGenweb Chatham Co, GA site.

He believes in Creatalytical Thinking and researching: the fusion of creativity and analysis to view life more fully and fulfill his place in this world. Writing now for over four decades, Marc has been influenced by history, science, art and relationships, and marvels at the cosmically-driven direction he receives each day from energy around him to record his ideas and research.